D0356592

Awakening the Soul

Awakening the Soul

A Book of Daily Devotions

EDITED BY
JOHN C. MORGAN

Skinner House Books

BOSTON

Copyright © 2001 by the Unitarian Universalist Association.
All rights reserved. Published by Skinner House Books, an imprint of the Unitarian Universalist Association, 25 Beacon Street, Boston, MA 02108-2800.

Printed in Canada

Cover design by Suzanne Morgan
Text design by Sandra Rigney

ISBN 1-55896-410-X

Library of Congress Cataloging-in-Publication Data
Awakening the soul: a book of daily devotions / edited by John C. Morgan.
    p. cm.
  ISBN 1-55896-410-X (alk. paper)
  1. Unitarian Universalist churches—Prayer-books and devotions—English. 2. Devotional calendars—Unitarian Universalist churches. I. Morgan, John C. (John Crossley), 1941–
BX9855.A84 2000
242'.2—dc21   00-063724

Acknowledgments on page 419.

10 9 8 7 6 5 4 3 2 1
03 02   01 00

All biblical passages cited are from the King James Version of the Bible.

The untitled poem by Nancy Ore for the December 1 devotion is from *Womanguides*, edited by Rosemary Radford Ruether © 1985 by Rosemary Radford Ruether. Reprinted by permission of Beacon Press, Boston.

Readers are invited to send comments about this devotional book to the editor at: John Morgan, First Unitarian Universalist Church of Berks County, 416 S. Franklin St., Reading, PA 19602.

The great end in religious instruction is . . . to awaken the soul, to excite and cherish spiritual life.

—WILLIAM ELLERY CHANNING, 1780–1842

PREFACE

Awakening the soul may at first seem a strange notion to a movement such as Unitarian Universalism, which appeared to be grounded in critical reason for at least the better part of the twentieth century. *Soul* was not a word often heard. Yet it was the parent of American Unitarianism, William Ellery Channing, who said that the great end of religion was precisely "to awaken the soul, to excite and cherish spiritual life." Some interpreters believe that one of the major reasons for the resurgence of our faith in the past decades has been our search for common spiritual ground and our deepened understanding that, while religion has an intellectual quality, it also requires intuition and heart and community—and mostly soul. In a movement that has been preoccupied with rationalism, awakening the soul is not so strange a concept after all.

"Soul" is an elusive quality, not easily defined. You know soul in a person or community when you feel it. The soul, as Carl Jung says, is the "archetype of life," the mystery encountered in the everyday experiences of living, the depth seen when you are present at the birth of a baby or when you hear music that touches you deeply, or when you look into the eyes of your beloved. In older days, pastors were seen as "caretakers of the soul." For much of the later part of the last century, therapy supplanted pastoral care and the "psyche" was addressed rather than the soul. In this light, it is not surprising that the soul needs to be awakened.

Awakening the Soul was inspired by *Day Unto Day*, a book of daily devotions published at the end of the nineteenth century by the American Unitarian Association. This devotional book is intended as a spiritual resource for nurturing your soul. What is truly personal is also truly universal. If we sit and wait for what is holy and deep, even if we don't use traditional theist language, our lives and the lives we touch are deepened and made ready. Jung was right: "Bidden or not bidden, God is present." Where you touch the Holy, it reaches to touch you, and your life will be transformed. If enough of us begin with our own spiritual disciplines, a whole community may be transformed, or a neighborhood or city or nation.

There is no need to wait until January 1 to begin using this book. You can begin today and keep going through all fifty-two weeks in this book. Set aside as best you can one time of the day for using this guide—whether ten minutes in the morning, or over lunch, or at bedtime. Read the selections slowly and pause as you feel the need to do so. Pray or stay in silence as you are moved to do so. Find a location where you feel comfortable and can find some moments away from disruptions. You may find that you need to be with others as you deepen your discipline. If so, find a group or start one.

The devotions here come from many spiritual traditions, reflective of some of the diversity in our midst. The contributors are Buddhists, Christians, mystics, pagans, humanists, and others who draw from multiple traditions. At the same time, the historic Jewish and Christian roots of Unitarian Universalism have not been overlooked. Without roots, it is hard to grow.

As you begin your devotional life, let this be your guide:

> In the end, it won't matter how much you have, but rather how much you have given.
>
> It won't matter how much you know, but rather how much you love.
>
> And it won't matter how much you profess to believe, but rather how deeply you live the few enduring truths you claim as ultimate.
>
> All the rest is discipline.

—JOHN C. MORGAN

Awakening the Soul

A WAKENING the soul requires that we pay attention to our imaginations and intuitions as well as our intellects and responsibilities. This is how we grow spiritually. Too often, we demand of ourselves only that we pay attention to the facts of life and we ignore imaginative engagement with the facts. Imaginative engagement is the soul's playground, and playfulness is a frequently unacknowledged spiritual discipline. "The reason angels can fly," writes G.K. Chesterton, "is that they take themselves so lightly." The less playful we are, the less chance there will be for grace and lightness of being to come into play.

JANUARY 1

Does this path have a heart? If it does, the path is good; if it doesn't, it is of no use.... One makes for a joyful journey; as long as you follow it, you are one with it. The other will make you curse your life. One makes you strong; the other weakens you.

—CARLOS CASTENEDA

Does the path I am following have heart? ～

May I walk the soulful journey. May I walk the journey with heart. May I have the courage to walk with the strength of my convictions. May I have the clarity to know my heart's soundings. May I have the vision and patience to walk one step at a time, knowing that each step holds eternity.

JANUARY 2

Imagination is the soul's playground.

How often do I let my imagination play? ⁓

May my soul be open to a soulful journeying. May I see hidden things. May I find awe in the moment. May delight and joy fill me with my soul's divine play.

JANUARY 3

Buddhists often speak of mindfulness. The Westerner
can easily conclude that to be mindful is to be rational
and logical, to use the analytical mind to figure things
out. Yet Buddhists mean something closer to soulful-
ness, in which one becomes aware of the hidden and
deeper meanings that reside in our everyday moments.
To pay attention to these moments and to act from that
awareness is soulfulness.

What insights would a soulful approach provide that are
missed when we try to figure things out? ⌁

May I become aware of those moments of joy residing in
a small child's hand in mine, in the play of sunlight
through leaves, in an understanding friend, in each and
every instant. May this awareness and joy make my life a
dance!

JANUARY 4

"Call the world, if you please,
The veil of Soulmaking.
Then you will find out
The use of the world."

—JOHN KEATS

What wider perspective would my life have if I saw the experiences of my life—the painful as well as the joyful and the mundane—as ways to stretch my soul into deeper understandings and a more encompassing compassion? ⌒

Stretch me, mold me, O Sacred Life, into shapes that express the heart of my life. Pull me, despite my fear, into a deeper heart space. Form my life into a more holy shape.

JANUARY 5

If we seek to understand the meaning of living a
soulful life, we will miss the mark, for the soul cannot
be understood. Soulfulness is a way of living with
heartfulness.

How would my life be transformed if it were driven by
heartfulness? How would it become infused with love if
I sought always to meet life with a heartful response to
myself and others? ⌣

O God, help me to find the deep kernel of truth you
have planted in my soul. May it be held and moistened
by the heartfulness of my living. May that kernel find
root in me, so divine love will grow from what you
placed there.

JANUARY 6

The heart creates images that color our lives. Heartful-
ness shapes a life of emotional richness and depth.
Jalaloddin Rumi wrote: "Sit at the image-house of the
heart, behold each painting we drew! One by One we
send new paintings so that the first may become the
second's morsel. . . . / I said to my heart, 'How are you?' /
It said, 'Increasing, for, by God, I am His Image's
House.'"

Can I remember a time when I was living from my heart
and the world was vibrant and alive—perhaps a time
when I was in love, or when I was experiencing change
or difficulty? 〜

Just as I color my world with my heart's images, may I
know each and every moment that some mysterious
Deep colors me. May I become aware of that Deep. May
I know it creates me. May I know it fills me and grows
me. May I know it loves me. O mysterious Deep, empty
my soul into the "Allness of the Universe."

A boy of that age when one begins to ask, Who am I and what is my place in all of this? was listening to his teacher describe the vastness of the universe—the solar system, the Milky Way galaxy, the local super-cluster of galaxies, the clusters of galaxies beyond clusters. Images of stars and galaxies came racing through the boy's mind as if he were on a spaceship moving through the universe. He became lost in the awe of it all. When his teacher asked him a question, he had to admit that he had no idea what she had asked. "Stop daydreaming," the teacher berated the boy, "and pay attention. You'll never go anywhere in life if you keep looking out the window all the time." The teacher, though, was unaware that the boy was paying attention—not to the curriculum of the class-room, but to the curriculum of the soul.

What flights of imagination are my soul's curriculum? ⌒

Imagine that you are a child again sitting in a classroom. Imagine yourself being transported from the classroom on a journey of wonder and discovery. Notice where you go. Sit for awhile with nothing but the intent of engaging your imagination. If images do not come to you, let your thoughts transport you. If thoughts do not come, let your feelings transport you. Now close your eyes and journey!

HOPE HELPS US to stretch into and out of ourselves as individuals and in community. We sometimes use hope to hold ourselves hostage, however, setting up expectations and clinging tightly to the way we think things should be. We should aim instead to be in a state of *hope without expectation* and then be grateful for what is created in that opening. In offering space for creation we become a part of all that is.

JANUARY 8

A primary offspring of Spirit is the evolving awareness of hope.

What would my life be like without hope? ⁓

May the stillness I have allowed myself, right here, right now, light the path for Creation to enter; and may I allow myself the seeing to know and welcome it into my life when it reveals itself.

JANUARY 9

Traditionally, Universalists believed that a loving God would not condemn a divinely created being to the eternal flames of hell. The Calvinists who dominated the time insisted that the vast majority of human beings are irredeemable and would be damned.

When did I last experience hope beyond what I was told was the truth? ⁓

May the love that is hope be tenderly nurtured in me such that it may transform despair in one other person today.

JANUARY 10

Hope lives somewhere between optimism and pessimism, informed by both but more clearly drawn to the positive.

What is one thing in my life that pulls hope toward the negative? ∼

Silence the head. Silence the heart. I am fresh. I am new. Let hope fill me up and liberate my spirit.

JANUARY 11

"Universalist wisdom posits that hope and despair are like Siamese twins, inextricably linked, and when torn asunder, both wither."

—CLARENCE SKINNER

In what way does my despair feed my hope? ∼

Power of my despair, embrace all sides of my being and show me how to take your wisdom softly into the world.

JANUARY 12

Hope is a world of possibility—a place of no achievable, measurable results; no goals; no place to get to.

What possibility can I offer to the world? ∼

Mystery and wonder, fill me up with the gentle Spirit of Life. Reach into my heart. Open me wide. Open me to speak what I see. Open me to make real what I am called to do in this world.

JANUARY 13

*Hope is not rational. The nature of hope is the ebb
and flow of energy where the soul speaks every
unknown language.*

Have I ever done anything that I could not prove was the
right thing to do? How did that feel? ∼

Blessed heart, be open to being touched by Spirit. Be
light and be respectful of what you know to be so. May
the force that moves through you be also affirmed. May
it be so in the simplest of all ways. In the gentle touch
of truth. In that uneducated dwelling spot you make
your home.

JANUARY 14

Universalism is often referred to as the "larger hope."
If we are, as the seventh Unitarian Universalist
Principle indicates, an interdependent web of all
things, everything *must be cherished, acknowledged,*
respected, nurtured, empowered.

What quality do I value most in myself and in others? ⁓

In this place of prayer and meditation, let me feel every
bone. Every molecule. Every blood vessel. Every heart-
beat. Every nerve ending. Everything. Let me know
it deeply. Let me connect it to others and all creations
deeply. Let me be in total and complete awe. Let me
smell. Let me hear. Let me hurt. Let me forgive. Let me
connect. Let me surrender. Let me marvel. Let me simply be amazed. Therein, let there be hope.

SOMETIMES CHILDREN of the Enlightenment, with their strong focus on reason, have a difficult time with traditional terms such as *faith*, *hope*, and *miracle*. Yet most persons have experienced faith as trust, hope as courage, and miracle as new opportunity. Nowhere is faith more evident than in the strange and seemingly miraculous meeting of Rev. John Murray, Universalism's founder, and an illiterate nonsectarian farmer by the name of Thomas Potter.

Potter, who lived in what is now Ocean County, New Jersey, had probably been visited by missionaries from the Ephrata Cloister in Pennsylvania, who were proclaiming the gospel of Universalism: that God's love is unlimited. So convinced was Potter of this truth that in 1760 he built a small meetinghouse along the Quaker lines for a Universalist preacher he believed would one day come to preach.

Having fled England after the deaths of his wife and son, John Murray wanted no part of sermons again. But in September of 1770, by a strange series of circumstances, Murray came to find Potter and his chapel and to preach a Universalist sermon. If "faith is the substance of things hoped for, the evidence of things not seen" (Hebrews 11:1), Thomas Potter's faith was such.

JANUARY 15

"Come, my friend. . . . I have longed to see you. I have been expecting you for a long time."

—THOMAS POTTER
(upon seeing John Murray for the first time)

What are the differences between believing in the future and believing the future in? What future that I have "longed to see" might I help believe into being? ∿

Help me to trust in what I cannot often see but feel deeply and intuit as truthful, and to hope for what is not yet, and to believe the future in.

JANUARY 16

"A few short weeks since I was in the most enviable circumstances.... Now I was alone in the world; no wife, no child... no home; nothing but the ghosts of my departed joys."

—JOHN MURRAY
(after the deaths of his wife and child and
shortly before he was put in debtor's prison)

Has my life ever been turned upside down so that I felt without hope? ∽

God of the hidden depths of our souls, help me when I have nowhere else to turn and give me strength for the facing of losses, that I might be comforted.

JANUARY 17

*"I determined to finish my wretched existence . . . but
in the moment of executing my fatal . . . purpose, the
image of my Eliza, irradiating the prison walls,
seemed to stand before me. She appeared as if com-
missioned by Heaven to sooth my tortured spirit . . .
and I was relieved."*

—JOHN MURRAY

Have I ever experienced moments seemingly "out of time,"
moments when my life has been transformed? ⌣

When all seems lost and I feel alone, help me to remember that there is yet One who abides with me, even to
the end of time.

JANUARY 18

"I was pleased with the wonders . . . of God as I beheld them in the great deep. I was astonished at the number of birds, flitting over the ocean. . . . On a brilliant moonlight evening our ship struck something. . . . We were in the center of the Western ocean. We soon discovered it was a sleeping whale. . . . Thus was my wondering mind beguiled of its sorrows."

—JOHN MURRAY
(en route to America, 1770)

Has the sight of the sky or mountains, the sound of the sea or birds, the fragrance of flowers, or the touch of a hand ever reawakened me to life and lifted me out of depression? ⁓

God of all creation, let me open my senses every day to your creation so that I might understand my place in it and experience the joy of life's dance.

JANUARY 19

*"I am unable either to read or write, but I am capable
of reflection; the sacred scriptures have been often
read to me, from which I gather that there is a great
and good Being, to whom we are indebted for all we
enjoy, . . . and as He had given me a house of my own,
I conceived I could not do less than to open it to strangers. . . . God . . . has put it into my heart to build this
house."*

—THOMAS POTTER
(to John Murray)

When was the last time I showed kindness to a stranger
without expecting anything in return? ∽

Let the light of gratitude shine in my heart, that I might
share what I have willingly with others who have need of
me.

JANUARY 20

"I discovered that if there be a ruling power, a super-intending providence, the account, given by the extraordinary man under whose roof I reposed, evinced its operation."

—JOHN MURRAY
(speaking of Thomas Potter)

Has a "ruling power" or "superintending providence" ever touched my life? ⌣

Creative Providence, let me be open to the working of your will on my life, that I may discover you still at work on your creation.

JANUARY 21

"He showed you by his life what it was to glorify God in body and spirit."

—JOHN MURRAY
(speaking of Thomas Potter)

In what ways does my life reflect my faith? ∼

Let my life speak as much as my words about what I truly value.

LOVE SOMETIMES SEEMS so intangible and amorphous that we cannot grasp it conceptually. We feel love as an emotion and we say we can describe it intellectually, but sometimes we only understand love as an action or a behavior. It is sometimes easier to love the world as an abstraction than to love one's partner or children or neighbor, yet it is precisely the concrete and visible expression of love that enables us to realize its power. To act out of love is to will that love to be present, first in ourselves but then for others. Experiencing love, we later reflect on its mystery.

JANUARY 22

Most of us have something we believe in deeply and wish to see manifest in the world. And all of us have had the experience of becoming critical or impatient with others because of a problem or lack in our spiritual communities, our neighborhoods, our schools, or our workplaces. But how many of us act *on our concerns and beliefs?*

What can I do to bring forth into the world what I yearn to see? ⌇

Before the Creator of all life, I vow to share broadly my unique spirit, which yearns to express itself within creation.

JANUARY 23

Looking within our own hearts, we can find ways to act in the world with our unique radiance—ways that will enrich the world for others. Hesitation due to fear of failure or lack of being perfect blocks our gifts to the world.

Will I choose to act upon my deepest beliefs and hopes for the world, or will I hold back due to fear? ⌣

All-Loving Spirit, with your never-ending encouragement and ever-present source available to me, I will embrace my path and act on my convictions.

JANUARY 24

People who excel in expression of their love for the world give us a great gift. We need to acknowledge this before them, letting them know that we revere what they offer us.

Do I take the time to praise and thank those who inspire me as I travel my path? ∼

Humbled before Your Spirit in the presence of strong people who devote themselves with uncommon might, I will practice a life of deep commitment to my beliefs. I will learn to express gratitude to those who teach and mentor me along the way.

JANUARY 25

*When we act upon our boldest dreams and commit
ourselves to our ideals, we are setting an example for
the world to behold. Those who witness the way we
translate our ideas into action will have the chance to
learn from us and do the same themselves.*

Can I see that setting an example for others is a gift to
the world? ⌣

God, help me shine with your light so that others
may learn to do the same. May I never underestimate
the power of holding to my convictions before my
community.

JANUARY 26

The circle of love grows as we love one another, for then love is shared.

In whom or what do I place my trust? ⁓

Bend my will, God, so that I may be transformed.

Every day we make a multitude of decisions about how to live, how to spend our time, how to relate to others, how to help others, how to tap into the spirit of the Creator. Each decision process takes varying degrees of thought before action results. Some decisions are relatively easy to make—for example, when to practice the piano or what to eat for breakfast. Those decisions that are harder—for example, deciding whether or not to risk our safety by helping a stranger, or deciding to commit time to a cause whose schedule conflicts with that of our regular commitments—can be informed by listening deeply to our intuition and praying/talking with the Creator.

Do I take time to bring my deepest self and the Creator into my decision-making process? ∼

Great Heart of the Creator, shine upon me your loving guidance as I open my heart to your word as it relates to my deeds. With your help and support, I can spread your light to others and share your blessings in this world.

JANUARY 28

If you have a desire to be a leader, learn to be a great
follower. When you follow, you listen, evaluate,
suggest ideas, and support the leader. You work with
people and ideally bring out the best in others as you
collaborate on tasks and responsibilities. The inspira-
tion and insight gained from everyone working
together bring great power to a group and its mission.

Do I take the time to appreciate, support, and inspire
those who lead me in various activities in my life? ∿

God, help me open my heart and mind to the greater
togetherness in supporting your mission on earth. Help
me to see how this will inform me for the times I myself
will lead. Teach me to respect and cherish those who
support me in my leadership responsibilities.

SOMETIMES CONFUSION about our faith is a way to hide a fear that there might be a common vision, at least in that part of our tradition called Universalism. Sometimes our diversity is not as diverse as we like to profess. And sometimes it is helpful to realize that until the twentieth century, Universalists did share a sense of what was at the heart of their faith. Whether we decide to incorporate the historic Universalist faith into our own is up to each person, but it is important to come to terms with what that faith was before keeping or discarding it. The unexamined faith is not worth living.

JANUARY 29

"In the 200 years since the group of people who called themselves Universalists... gathered in... Oxford, Massachusetts,... the denomination they were unknowingly creating has evolved in ways that would have amazed and perhaps disturbed them.... Nevertheless, the strong thread of history runs uninterrupted... binding them and perhaps present-day Unitarian Universalists firmly together in the shared affirmation of a Love that transcends both time and place."

—CHARLES HOWE

What is the core affirmation or value I affirm as a Unitarian Universalist? ∼

Spirit of Truth, which is discovered in the present moment but also transcends both time and place, keep me mindful of my heritage, open to the possibility that my vision may be limited by my own insistence that I am right and those who differ are wrong, and deeply humbled by the evolving dynamics of new understandings. Keep me mindful and kindhearted.

JANUARY 30

"The foundation of democracy is the realization that every human being is a child of God..., always trusting in the one God which ever lives and loves."

—OLYMPIA BROWN

How do I (or should I) act on the core value that every human being has worth and dignity or is a child of God? ∼

God of our troubled lives, help me to live as a person of integrity who acts as if every person has infinite worth. Though I falter and fail, keep fresh before my mind and heart the desire to be a healing presence.

JANUARY 31

"Preach the Universal and Everlasting Gospel of Boundless, Universal Love for the entire human race, without exception.... Proclaim and publish to the people of the word a Universal Gospel that shall restore, in time, all the human species.... The inner Spirit makes us feel that behind every appearance of diversity there is an interdependent unity of all things."

—GEORGE DE BENNEVILLE

In what ways am I like other people? ⌇

When I think that I am better than other people, remind me of my weaknesses and faults. And when I complain of others, remind me of their complaints against me, that I may learn to walk humbly and with compassion for myself and others.

FEBRUARY 1

"Universalism conveys the reproof that we all have a common origin, a common end, a common relation to God."

—GEORGE ROGERS

What are the insights of my faith that inspire me to share it with others? ⌒

When I believe that I am better than others, remind me of my own shortcomings so that I may learn humility and practice kindness.

FEBRUARY 2

*"Such a heterogeneous gathering assembled as can
hardly be imagined, made up . . . of Christian
Unionists proper, Perfectionists, Transcendentalists,
Comeouters, and nondescript eccentrics of widely
varying types. . . . The parties . . . found themselves so
involved in erratic and chaotic opinionists that they
had hard work to control the proceedings."*

—ADIN BALLOU
(describing an 1840 conference called
to discuss Christian unity)

Where is the source of the unity of spirit in my spiritual
community? ⌣

In the midst of confusion and clutter, teach me to listen
for that still, small voice that speaks of unity and clarity
and wholeness in a broken and loud world.

FEBRUARY 3

A priceless way to reflect God's love in the world is to share our spiritual beliefs and thoughts with others who also desire to commune spiritually. Our spiritual essence grows deeper simply by our articulation of personal beliefs. Listening to others express their own spiritual thoughts, practices, and commitments allows us to listen on a very deep level to another soul. We are meant to help one another in our quest for meaning and grace.

Have I considered sharing my spiritual life in a community setting? Do I take the time to listen to the spiritual yearnings of others? ～

God, help me to see that I can share your love with the world by sharing my spirituality with others. Help me also to listen deeply to my fellow beings as they share their own spiritual life with me.

FEBRUARY 4

Love is stronger than death. Death has its moments in our lives and in history, but death does not have the last word. It is not easy to speak of love when death seems dominant. But if love is not stronger than death, then those we cherish the most are wrong. Martin Luther King, Jr., killed fighting for the rights of garbage workers, was wrong; Jesus and Gandhi were wrong; Jim Reeb and Olympia Brown were wrong. We cannot accept this. Even though life seems unfair and all too short, it is better to live as if love is stronger than death. This understanding is the essence of our common faith as Unitarian Universalists.

Have I ever felt that death is unjust and love too deep to be lost forever? ∿

May the joy of the morning light and the strength of the eternal hills and the calm of the evening light fading into the new day be in my heart and with all those I love, now and until we meet again.

L IFE IS FILLED with new beginnings. There is a hope that comes with each new day and each new possibility for a new beginning. Perhaps we are all looking for Eden, the primal community, the place where everything began. But the reality is that none of us really begin anew, free of past behaviors, errors of judgment, mistakes. If we are to be free of the past, we must first acknowledge that it remains with us if we have not comes to terms with it. We need to accept our mistakes, learn from them, and be ready to move on. Only in this way can we really move on.

FEBRUARY 5

Life is a matter of beginnings and endings; its rhythms ebb and flow. But there is "music" in beginnings, new energy, and the creative impulse is free to roam.

How do I greet new beginnings? ∼

Let my heart and mind be filled with hope and optimism as I begin something new today.

FEBRUARY 6

Beginning something new can be terrifying, particularly if we do not appear to have a natural predilection for succeeding. Sometimes we just have to suspend our self-doubt and take a leap of faith, the way a child does when he or she jumps into a swimming pool for the first time. As the journalist known for his passion for running, John "The Penguin" Bingham, writes, "The miracle isn't that we finish, the miracle is that we have the courage to start."

How do I find the strength to begin something new? ∽

I will focus on what I want to accomplish and not allow my fears to hold me back.

FEBRUARY 7

In his book Pragmatism, *William James wrote, "We live in a world uncertain to be saved. . . . [A]re you willing to take the risk of participating in such a world?"*

Where do I seek the courage to take risks and try something different? ∼

May I believe in myself enough to believe in the world.

FEBRUARY 8

Welcoming newcomers often requires us to step outside our comfort zones. If we accept the recommendation of Jesus and others that we become like children, the task of welcoming becomes easier. Consider this: When a family moves into a new home, the neighborhood children often invite the new children to join them at play almost immediately.

Do I welcome and encourage people new to my neighborhood or my circle of friends? What about newcomers to my congregation or my workplace? ∼

Let me reach out to others who are new, just as I would want others to reach out to me.

FEBRUARY 9

*Religious conservatives often say that the story of Sodom
and Gomorrah is a condemnation of homosexuality.
That is a naive reading. The real story is about the
mistreatment of strangers, those who are different
from ourselves. If we take the story to heart, it will
alter our dealings with strangers.*

How do I welcome people who are different from
myself? Do our differences hold me back from reaching
out to them? ⌣

May I have the courage to see beyond differences and to
recognize the similarities in those who are new to me.

FEBRUARY 10

*How precious, yet how fragile, is the gift of life. So
too our connections to the whole of it, past and
present—here now and then gone. How delicate,
tragic, majestic, and beautiful* each *life is—full of
wonder and of terror.*

When do I feel the deepest about life? ⁓

The circle of your love grows, O God, as we love life in
all its brevity and power.

Legend has it that Bill Russell, who was the ultimate team leader of the ultimate basketball team, the Boston Celtics, felt ill before every game. Although, with his long history in sports, one might have expected him to see his job as routine, he clearly saw it as filled with "new beginnings." We all face those same new beginnings as we teach in a classroom or work in a lab or police a neighborhood or build a house.

What new beginnings do I dread facing today? ⌣

Let me have the courage to face the new challenges that today will bring.

A PARISHIONER ONCE ASKED a group, "Why can't we pray?" After an uncomfortable silence, one man responded, "Because we don't believe in that stuff." But we know from research that prayer "works"; it can, for example, improve the well-being of a person facing illness or loss. Prayer "works" even for the most scientifically minded of us, because it touches a human being. We may be convinced that prayer doesn't change *events*, but we would have a more difficult time arguing that prayer doesn't change *people*. It does. And it may be that prayer also changes the reality with which it deals. The truth is that the only way to pray is to pray, not to *think* about praying.

FEBRUARY 12

"I would be silent and let infinity speak through me."
—ROBERT T. WESTON

What has been my experience with prayer? ⌇

Life of Life, deepest voice in my spirit, let me listen before speaking, sit quietly before reacting, hear what it is I am being asked to do before acting, and follow the teachings of my heart.

FEBRUARY 13

There will always be times when life seems flat and no deeper presence is felt. Mystics have called such times "dark nights of the soul." During such times, even the sounds of birds are perceived as cries for help. But remember the wisdom of the ages: "Don't be afraid. Have patience and trust. You are not alone."

When was my last "dark night of the soul"? ⌒

Absent God, Presence not felt, help me to wait without idols, quietly remembering how you have touched my life and been the source of my inner strength.

FEBRUARY 14

"Ask and it shall be given you; seek, and ye shall find;
knock, and it will be opened unto you."

—MATTHEW 7:7

We often hear these words of caution: "Be careful what
you pray for. You may get it." What do these words
mean? ⌣

Guide to the Future, which enters space but lives
beyond time, help me to become all that I know is best
and to live all that I feel is true, so that my life unfolds
as a blessing for others.

FEBRUARY 15

In prayer we open our hearts to the deepest layer of what it means to be human, and in that process we are transformed by a power beyond the human.

When was the last time I felt a power beyond the human? ∼

Living Presence, which has touched my life in so many ways, stay in touch. Often I forget your power and need to be disturbed in order to feel you again, as if for the first time.

FEBRUARY 16

"I have spent my life searching for a reality fit to be worshipped. Last night I woke up and decided it didn't make any difference."

—REMARK MADE AT QUAKER WORSHIP MEETING

What difference does it make if I spend my life searching for a reality fit to be worshipped? ∼

Power that runs ahead of me, slow me down, that I may listen to your presence in my life and help me to understand that the deepest questions of my heart are the clues to a reality fit to be worshipped.

FEBRUARY 17

"Today we are not dependent on any text or the letter of any book. It is the spirit that giveth life and the spirit speaks to our souls."

—OLYMPIA BROWN

When have I felt most alive, most in communion with my deepest self and with that which transcends self? ∼

Spirit that lives in all creation yet is beyond the decay of time, stay with me today, that I might learn to love myself and others.

FEBRUARY 18

*It is not out of self-satisfaction that we pray, nor do
we pray out of abundance. Rather, we pray out of
need. We pray as losers, because this describes who we
are when the masks are down. And when we understand this, even our wounds are gifts.*

How can wounds be gifts? Can I appreciate any of my
own wounds in that light? ⌒

Mask down, wounds exposed, heart open, I come before
myself and God vulnerable and without props. Let me
feel loved as I am, not for what I do.

THE WORDS OF the liturgy, as familiar and comforting as a child's much-loved blanket, help us get in touch with our deepest selves, the people we treasure, and the Holy. The words we are used to saying to each other as the service begins feel as familiar and sacred as the liturgy itself. *Good morning*—an affirmation of creation. *Hello*—an acknowledgment of other. *Peace be with you*—a hope for the wellness of one's soul. We customize our greetings, wanting to be appropriate to the context. We protect ourselves from possible embarrassment or rejection by keeping a formality at times.

*"Peace be with you." Many times when we attend
worship, peace is definitely not with us. On such
occasions, having the priest or other officiant wish it
to the participants and the participants wish it back
to the priest can feel very personal and very right.
Such a greeting seems to acknowledge that peace is
not an automatic response, that peace is not to be
taken for granted, and that peace is a necessary ingre-
dient of the soul. "Peace be with you."*

Whom would I like to wish "peace" to? ∼

May peace surround me as I enter this day. May peace
fill my breath and my life, helping me to set aside fear
and anger, helping me to feel every day an at-oneness.
May peace be with those I love, with my neighbors, with
the world.

FEBRUARY 20

*The Prayers of the Faithful or Petitionary Prayers of
the Catholic Church name groups of people or situations in general ways for God to consider—for
example, "For all the depressed, the ill, the homebound, and the addicted." The list rotates—praying
for lawyers one week, teachers another—but the
congregational response is the same: "Lord, hear our
prayer." The people say it together, politely, as if to say,
"Me too." Sometimes we would sooner shout the
response, demand an audience, or grovel and beg:
"God, please listen. You are hearing me, right?" We
learn that we are not in charge, we cannot set the
holy agenda, and we cannot make these demands. But
still, we can say, politely, "Lord—please—hear our
prayer."*

What do I want God to hear? ∼

Dear God, let these prayers remind me that I am very
much like other people—including the depressed, the ill,
the homebound, the addicted. Let me remember that I
am not different from the most broken and that my self-
reliance serves no one well.

This forgiveness business is a difficult thing. Forgiving us as we forgive others—to the extent that we do forgive—seems like harsh scorekeeping. It's as if to say, "Don't come crying to me about your human frailty if you don't recognize that others also have human frailty." Forgiveness is never presented as an option *(forgive only those whom you feel like forgiving); it's always a blanket expectation. Recognizing that although forgiveness can take time, it needs to be the ultimate goal, one wise soul always puts "trespass" in the past tense when praying the Lord's Prayer: "...as we forgive those who trespassed against us."*

Whom do I need to forgive? ∽

Grant that I may be forgiven—that, like a debt of money owed, the slate of my errors may be wiped clean. Grant me the grace to forgive those who have erred against me. We are only imperfect human creatures.

FEBRUARY 22

Some of us grew up saying the Lord's Prayer straight through, beginning with "Our Father" and not stopping until the final "Amen" has been uttered. In the Catholic church, the people stop and the priest interjects some words about peace and protection from all anxiety. Some priests say "from all needless *anxiety," perhaps acknowledging that anxiety is a condition hard to avoid in this lifetime. But even if anxiety is inevitable, we can seek protection from it: that it not be overwhelming, that we feel safe even in the face of anxiety, that we not isolate ourselves but stay in touch with our spiritual resources when we are anxious.*

Under what circumstances do I feel protected from anxiety? ∼

Find me a mantra to get me through the night, when the storms are strong and the fears run high. Find me a song to calm my soul, to join me to a Greater Presence when anxiety won't leave. Find me a prayer to open my heart and know it will be okay.

Mercy *is one of those words used so many ways as to be confusing. Many healing institutions have taken the name Mercy Hospital. "Mercy!" was a favorite exclamation of an older generation. And some expressions of mercy seemed related to God: "It's a mercy he survived," someone might say, or "Have mercy." Sometimes we confuse mercy with pity, and then our pride can get in the way. "Kind and compassionate treatment" is what one dictionary says.*

And yet when we hear the words "Have mercy on us" in church, the precise definition is less important that the resonance we feel: Yes (our hearts sing), have mercy on us. *We mess up. We fall short. We even do things incredibly wonderfully right sometimes. But have mercy on us, because we will not be able to do things incredibly wonderfully right every time.*

Where do I need mercy in my life? ∽

Merciful God, help me to understand my humanity. Help me to know that I will need mercy from time to time. Kindness and compassion—mercy—can heal my life. Kindness and compassion—mercy—can hold me in love. Have mercy on us.

FEBRUARY 24

*We give thanks this day for our daily bread and
wonder at all we have seen going by another path,
returning to our home, and going out into the world
to tell of all we have seen.*

*We are all the child, the wisemen, the virgin
mother, the father of that we did not father, fleeing
into exile, to a foreign land, returning to our ministry,
overturning the economics of worship, and teaching a
new commandment to fulfill a prophecy of long ago.*

What parts of this story am I living out? Is this what I
want to be doing with my one precious life? ∽

O Lord, help me see the story of my life and its author.

Those of us who attend Mass are sent forth from worship with these words: "Go in peace, to love and to serve our God." It is not a simple task we are asked to do. We struggle to find a sense of peace. We forget to love God. We forget, even, to serve God. How can we forget when we are reminded so often? Still, it is hard for us to keep that focus of love and service, that focus of peace. Maybe we have to hear the words more often—more than a hundred times, more than three hundred times, more than five hundred times—before they "take."

Go in peace, to love and to serve our God.

What can I do to keep the focus in my life? ∿

Peace. Love. Service. These are not hard concepts. Help me to fill my life with them. Help me to know that these are enough. Peace. Love. Service.

EVANGELISM SIMPLY MEANS sharing your good news with others. This requires, of course, that you know what the good news is. What is it about your faith that has sustained you, transformed your life, given you hope? If your faith has affected you deeply, you cannot help but share it with others. Evangelism does not mean telling others how to live or what to believe, but helping them to see by your life and words what it is you hold as most important.

FEBRUARY 26

Rev. George Rogers (1804–1846) was a tireless and
energetic evangelist on the frontiers of American life.
Converted to Universalism in an African-American
church in Philadelphia, Rogers took to the open
road throughout many states and into Canada. In
Pittsburgh, Pennsylvania (where he claimed to be the
first Universalist preacher to speak openly), some in
the crowd threw rocks at him. He said, "Let me tell
you, my friends, you have mistaken your man. I am
not thus to be stopped: I would preach the love of
God at the martyr's stake."

In what or whom do I place trust? ∼

In the midst of struggle and suffering, help me to find
strength for living and to bear witness to that strength in
all that I say or do.

FEBRUARY 27

"As I looked out over the large congregation, and observed the rapt delight which beamed in almost every countenance, I was forced to own that the religion which could thus sway and felicitate that mass of individuals...would be degraded by a comparison with the cold and barren abstractions of infidel philosophy."

—GEORGE ROGERS
(after attending the service at which
he was "restored to Christianity")

When was the last time my heart was moved in a worship service? ⌇

Deepest Reality, which lives in us to stir our souls and make us dissatisfied with all the dead forms of faith, let me be moved too, so that I might feel your presence.

FEBRUARY 28

*"I had now traveled over Ohio, in zig-zag directions
for a full four hundred miles....I have become seized
with a burning desire that it should become...a field
of Universalist labor."*

—GEORGE ROGERS

When was the last time I shared my deepest faith and
values with another person? ∼

Help me to hear the deepest prayers of others and to
share mine with others, lest I become a church of one.

MARCH 1

Rev. George Rogers was a man "short of stature,
roughly dressed, having great metal buttons on a coat
that might have fitted almost any other man as well—
a sadly worn white hat 'run to seed'—the other
extremity of his person being muddy shoes with the
strings untied."

—ABEL C. THOMAS

How might my congregation react if Rev. George Rogers
showed up on Sunday morning? 〜

God of our inner lives, teach me to look within a person
for what endures.

MARCH 2

*"Many an hour I have sat reading my Bible by the
side of some brook or at some log in the silent depths
of the forest, and in such situations, the soul can
enjoy more pure communion with the Creator. . . . O,
the woods! The interminable woods! And the ponds
and marshes and flooded flats in which the road is
perpetually losing itself to the infinite bewilderment
of the traveler."*

—GEORGE ROGERS

Where am I restored? ⌣

If I do not care for myself, my soul, no one else will.
Help me to practice the presence of the Holy in silence
and solitude, wherever I may be.

MARCH 3

*"I had borne the main brunt of the difficulties inci-
dent to the establishing of a church..., and to those
who have not experienced them, it is not easily con-
ceivable what those difficulties are....I had resigned
the pastoral care of that society; for, with the church
property to pay for, they were utterly unable to pay my
salary, and I was utterly unable to subsist without it."*

—GEORGE ROGERS
(on having to sell his house and books and leave
his pastoral charge in Cincinnati, Ohio)

Do I have a faith to sustain me when it appears that I
have failed? ⌢

Help me to understand that spiritual joy is not to be
measured by what others believe to be success, but that
the marks of joy are companionship, faith, hope, and a
sense of having worked and suffered for some great
transforming truth.

MARCH 4

*There are five principles of Universalism that
prompted Rogers's evangelism. He listed them as
follows: to teach God's love for all humanity, to draw
the human family together in love, to show that it is
pleasurable to do good, to give people hope, and to
show that there is no conflict between reason and
faith.*

What principles or values would prompt me to share my
life and faith with others? ⌒

Spirit of Truth, I know in my heart what it is that brings
me hope, but I often fail in my life to live that hope or
share it with others. Give me the courage to live and
speak the truths I know.

ONE UNITARIAN UNIVERSALIST called himself "a Unitarian of the Third Person." He was referring not to the Trinity, but to a recognition that the word "spirit" denotes the presence of some deep aspect of life in our own midst. When we speak of a "spirited discussion" or a "spirited person," we understand what the words mean. They point to life in all its heartfelt depth, connections with one another, passion and principle united—all more like a dance to which we are invited than a proposition to which we give our assent or disapproval. In the Latin, "spirit" simply means "breath," that invisible life force we see leave the body when it dies. Spirit is that which gives life its fullest purpose and meaning.

MARCH 5

A liberal Methodist theologian was teaching a seminary course in liberal theology to a group of Unitarian
Universalist seminarians. The theologian remarked
one day in class, "Of God, Christ, and the Holy
Spirit, Unitarian Universalists don't emphasize God
so much, nor Christ; rather, you UUs emphasize the
Holy Spirit. I have heard you call it by several
names—'the Spirit of Life,' 'the Sacred,' and 'the
Holy.' When you use those terms, you express what I
understand as the Holy Spirit."

Where in my life do I feel most connected to a sense of
the Sacred and the Holy? In what places? What experiences? What resonates for me when I express that
connection to the Sacred and Holy as the presence of
the Holy Spirit? ∼

Notice your breathing.
Your breathing is the breath that sustains.
Your breath is the in-breathing of the Holy.
Let it not be just air you breath in.
Rather, let it be the Spirit
That sustains and transforms all.
With each breath feel yourself being uplifted.
Now close your eyes and be attentive.

MARCH 6

When you are most anxious or in despair, when changes—whether wanted or unwanted—engulf you, when life seems too much to handle, you might feel as if you have stepped over the brink into an abyss. If you let go and trust the feeling of groundlessness, you will find an unknown, unexpected Presence lifting you.

Can I remember a time when I felt afraid, anxious, depressed; when I felt at the end of my ability to cope with life? Have I ever let go and trusted something beyond me or deeply inside me to lift and sustain me? If not, can I imagine such a time? ∽

O Source of life and healing, help me to know the wisdom of letting go of dead expectations, of shriveling anxieties, and in the letting go, may I see that my life is lifted and filled beyond my knowing.

MARCH 7

*A frequent motif in ancient legends about the births
of gods was the visit by a god or the spirit of a god to a
young woman who later gave birth to a savior. In
Christian tradition, the Holy Spirit visited Mary, and
Jesus Christ was born to save humankind with
redeeming love.*

What transformation and freedom could I find if I
allowed the Spirit of the Holy to know my most hidden
fear? Even if I am barely aware of it, it holds me back
from becoming the person I am meant to be. What healing would occur if I shared that secret or fear with the
Spirit of the Holy? What love would come forth from
me? What possibilities would be born? ～

Open me, O Spirit of Life. Here is my offering to you. I
hold nothing back. I offer you all I have—my experiences of living: all the times I have fallen short, all the
times I was grace-filled. Here they are—my fears, my
doubts, my anger, as well as my hopes, my convictions,
my joys. Take them. Transform them. And having given
you this, my offering, I await the rebirth of wonder.

MARCH 8

"God is our refuge and strength, a very present help in trouble. Therefore will not we fear though the earth be removed, and though the mountains be carried into the midst of the sea; though the waters thereof roar and be troubled, though the mountains shake.... 'Be still, and know that I am God.'"

—PSALM 46:1–3, 10

At times in my life when I have been "still"—maybe while in a natural setting, maybe while in prayer or meditation—have I noticed a peace move over me as my troubles and fears disappeared? If not, can I imagine such a peace? ∼

Let me be still! Let the peace of deep waters move over me. Let me be still! Let the presence of the Holy infuse me with the peace that is my birthright. Let me be still! Let me know that I am loved by a love that will not let me go.

MARCH 9

Jesus and his followers were on their way to Jerusalem for Passover. At one place along the way, Jesus drew his disciples together and told them how to remain faithful in the face of fear. Among other things, Jesus said to them, "And when they bring you unto the synagogues and unto magistrates, and powers, take ye no thought how or what thing ye shall answer, ... For the Holy Ghost shall teach you in the same hour what ye ought to say."

—LUKE 12:11–12

To what in my life do I give rule and authority that creates anxiety, worry, or concern for me? ∽

May I cast away my anxiety and worry about those who would judge me, for I have deep within me a holy voice that knows only love. Let me listen to this holy voice for it will speak only loving thoughts. Let me trust this voice of wisdom, for it will teach me only love.

A religious man lay near death in a hospital. A hospital chaplain asked if there was anything he could do. The man said, "Yes, there are two things. First, pray with me; the second I will tell you later." After they had prayed together, the man said, "My second request is that you call my son. I was strict with him when he was growing up. I'm afraid I hurt him. I need to ask his forgiveness before I die." The chaplain called the man's son, who poured out experiences to the chaplain of ridicule and blame from his father. Finally, the son said, "But I know he loves me in his way. I wish I could forgive him." The chaplain offered a silent prayer asking for wisdom. Then these words came— not from the chaplain but rather through him: "To forgive is to remember only the loving thoughts you've had for another and to remember only the loving thoughts that others have had for you."

Can I remember (or imagine) a time when words or motivation seemed to come through me rather than from me—as if I had been a conduit for holy wisdom? ⁓

O Spirit of Life, move through me, bringing wisdom, bringing love. Help me to know that life is grace-filled, brimming with blessings. May my eyes be opened so that I may see more clearly, my ears so that I may hear beyond words, and my heart so that I may know the depths of things.

People who live along the seacoast often find that life begins to move with the rhythms of the tides. The blue herons who fish nearby become companions. The gulls that fly inland each morning and seaward each evening mark their workday with that of the humans. On the eastern shores, the sun rising across the water is like a god announcing its presence each morning in a different garb—sometimes rose-colored from horizon to horizon, sometimes a ball of bold yellow light. And at night the moon lays a path of light across the water, inviting onlookers into reflection on the endless path of life continually arising. As we look on such a scene, we may know that the herons, the gulls, and we are cradled by a Goddess Spirit embracing us in a miracle beyond knowing.

What everyday miracles in my life leave me with a sense of the Divine Presence? What sacred, daily rhythms does this Presence bring to me? ⌒

Open me, O Spirit. Hold me in your embrace. My cares melt in the awe of your presence. Your touch tells me I am no orphan, rather a child of your huge heart.

HOW WE DEAL WITH suffering and outright evil tells us whether or not our faith has grown inside us deeply so as to supply strength and hope for living when life gets especially harsh. Some critics claim that a sunshine faith is fine for good times but will not provide resources for bad times, as when we lose a loved one or when illness descends on us. An onward-and-upward faith may suffice for those who are fortunate in terms of material goods or health, but it is not sufficient for those who are down and out, who have lost their reasons for living. When life is at its bleakest, inner resources are needed—resources nurtured over a lifetime of faith.

MARCH 12

"I then discovered the root of all my sins and iniquities within my heart. That discovery brought me into an extreme agony, and despair entered into my soul."

—GEORGE DE BENNEVILLE

When was the last time I felt hopeless? ⌒

Inner Light, shine on those parts of myself that I do not acknowledge before others—my shortcomings and sometimes willful words and actions that hurt others—and let me not pass by them without reflecting on my need to own responsibility for causing pain in others.

MARCH 13

*"I was about 17 years of age when I began to preach
in France. . . . We were many times taken prisoners
during the two years. . . . Many of us were hanged,
others whipped by the hands of the hangman and
branded with a hot iron."*

—GEORGE DE BENNEVILLE

If I were arrested for my faith, what evidence would be
used against me? ⌒

May I find the inner strength to live what I believe,
especially when I face loss.

MARCH 14

As George de Benneville's companion M. Durant was about to be hanged for his beliefs, he sang these words from Psalm 126: "They that sow in tears shall reap in joy."

When was the last time I cried, and for what reason? ∿

God of our captive years, release me from mourning, that I might rejoice once again in being alive.

MARCH 15

When George de Benneville was a young boy, he was sent to sea to learn discipline. While off the coast of Africa, he chanced to see a group of local men surrounding another stricken man and pointing to the sun. Demanding to know what was happening, he was told that one of the men had hurt his leg, and the others were praying for his recovery. De Benneville commented that these men were Christians and he, the heathen.

When was the last time I helped someone in need? ∽

Compassionate One, who dwells in every living being, help me to see that where one suffers, everyone suffers.

MARCH 16

"The weakness of my body increased so that I was certain of dying."

—GEORGE DE BENNEVILLE

How has death affected my life? ∽

Help me to live so that, when it comes time to die, my life will have been lived fully.

MARCH 17

"Dear soul, take courage, be comforted."

—GEORGE DE BENNEVILLE

When I am suffering emotionally, physically, or spiritually, what brings comfort and courage? ∼

Spirit of Comfort, which is as close as my breath and as near as my silence, bring to me a deeper sense of your love and companionship, that I might know whence I have come and where I am going.

MARCH 18

*"The fountain of grace bless and preserve thee,
and cause his face to shine upon and in thee, and
enlighten thy understanding both in time and
eternity."*

—GEORGE DE BENNEVILLE

What is a blessing? ∼

Bless my life and all that is within me, both in time and
eternity.

SELFLESSNESS APPEARS in our lives in two aspects, one a reflection of the other. In romantic love, in family life, in friendships, in society, we know without thinking that our relationships are meaningful and strong when we find ourselves willing to—happy to—give of ourselves in order that another may benefit and grow. Selflessness is the center of our social experience. Deeper still by far, selflessness is also the center of our very existence.

As the impulse to act in the interest of another rather than in one's own interest, selflessness is the heart of love. Selflessness and love may even be the same thing. It is said that if you love someone deeply enough, that person so fills your awareness that there is no room for thought of self.

When have I loved someone—or something—so deeply that all thought of myself vanished? ⌁

In the love of those closer to me than myself, let me burn off the impurities of self-centeredness, self-indulgence, and self-importance, to be free of all but that love and that which is required to sustain it.

MARCH 20

To act fully, responsively, and responsibly in the interest of another, selflessly, we have to begin from a vital sense of self. In order to be selfless—truly to love—we have to have a self of worth to give up and an identity of integrity in which to be grounded.

Have I ever been in a situation where I felt called upon (or impelled) to be selfless—and resented it? ⌒

Help me to embrace the qualities I sense to be good and make them part of me, to grow in strength and knowledge for my task, and to gain confidence to be able to hold on when it is appropriate and let go when it is time.

MARCH 21

In healthy, mature relationships, selflessness—love—flows from both directions, freely offered. We give all that we are able, expecting nothing in return—but still we know that we will get what we need to sustain us.

What would be my ideal in a loving relationship? ⌣

May I have the depth of soul to enter into the reality that the value of my life, and that of all others, lies in giving of the self—giving not for the sake of the receiver, or for one's own sake, but for the sake of the giving.

MARCH 22

Selflessness, in its full purity, is the absence *of self.
While* self *and* relationship *are constructs of time,
true selflessness is the direct experience of eternity, in
which nothing exists but Being itself.*

How do I feel about the idea that my self could cease to
exist, even for a moment? ∼

Allow that which is real to burst through the bounds of
my "knowing" and "understanding."

From those instants of selflessness that all of us are brought to at times throughout our days, most often unexpected and fleeting—instants of losing ourselves utterly in connectedness, in concentration, in inspiration, in creativity—springs all meaning in human life.

What are a few of the most intensely positive experiences in my life? ~

Burrow deep into the soil of my soul, Awareness, when I'm not looking, to surface once more suddenly—and make me look.

MARCH 24

Moments of timeless awareness, in which the self does not enter in, cannot be willed. Indeed, they are the opposite of will. But the ground can be prepared for them. Life can be lived such that they are more likely to come.

What might I do if I wanted to improve the quality of my life? ∼

Let my mind and spirit come to rest, from time to time, in joyous gratitude for existence, in humble recognition of the limits of human capacities, in steadying consciousness of the presence of a Being greater than myself.

*Being fully selfless is living as love. That state may
not be completely attainable, at least not at all times.
But we can strive for it wholeheartedly. Not to love
something or someone, but to love without subject or
object. To be love.*

What do I live for? ∿

May my every act, my every word, my very being
emanate in and as love from the one selfless core of all.

PRAYERFULNESS IS not just a habit of speaking words to some listening force out there. At its core, it is the process or act in which new relationships are established. What is "out there" begins "in here," within ourselves, and then reaches out to encompass our fellow human beings and all creation. Being prayerful shows reverence for all life, respect for differences and for the unity of being at the same time, openness to new understandings and humility about our short-sightedness, and a deep desire to feel connected to our selves, to others, and to that which is greater than self.

MARCH 26

As you begin this new day, creating order where there was none, breathing new life into your corner of the world, reflecting in rich silence, remember that you mirror the original day, when out of the void light was gathered; out of nonexistence, life; out of loneliness, relatedness. Keep this link fresh in your heart so that you might have no fear, knowing whence you have come, and where you are going.

Do I have any inner sense of where I came from and where I am going? ∼

Grant me an inner sense of feeling my link to all that has been and all that is and all that is to come.

When all seems lost, pray for the courage to continue, knowing that what you cannot see the Spirit of New Beginnings can see. Let the power of the future, hidden but already here, be present as a beacon to light the way.

Have I ever felt the future emerging in the present moment? ⌣

Help me to stay in the Eternal Now and understand that, in the depths, time is not measured by clocks.

The only way to pray is to pray, and not to think about praying.

What am I learning about practicing prayerfulness? ∽

In seeking, let me find; in searching, let me be found; in finding, let me discover God.

MARCH 29

*We cannot mirror the wide spectrum of love which
the Creator offers to the world. We share what we are
capable of at any given moment. There will be
moments when we feel unproductive or inexpressive
in our words and actions. Personal failure, or inability
to meet all goals with one-hundred-percent success, is
inevitable. Learning from our failures helps us to
refine and reset our course.*

Do I criticize myself too quickly, too often, for not achieving my goals with consistent, superior results? ~

God, help me to accept myself lovingly as I strive to do
your work in the world. Help me to be gentle and
patient with myself so that I may learn from my failures
and consider them as valuable as my successes in the
course of a lifetime.

MARCH 30

Where is God? We often ask this question during times of despair over what seems to be unfair claiming of lives.

Where is God? ∼

Spend five minutes in silent reflection.

MARCH 31

We can be grateful today for our unbelief: for refusing to accept the truths handed us, for struggling against prevailing orthodoxies, for seeking truth that has meaning for us.

What were the major truths presented to me as a child? ∼

In the midst of my rebellion and resistance, help me to remember those truths that still have meaning over time, deepened by experience and wisdom and hope.

APRIL 1

God, this is a struggle you have called us to be in. You need us as much as we need you, not to spout the correct doctrine or to belong to the right religion, but to feel your presence, do justice in the world, and to love creation with all our hearts, minds, and actions.

When, if ever, have I felt God's presence? ⁓

Make quiet the rehearsed prayer, keep still my soul, that I may listen with my heart to you, O God, and no longer be afraid. So let me listen.

HUMAN BEINGS are fallible creatures. That is a given. Hardly a day goes by that we do not hurt someone we care for; and we ourselves are often hurt as well. Given our history of failures—large and small—it is no wonder that forgiveness is crucial to our well-being. Yet despite all the practice we have had, granting (and accepting) forgiveness remains a challenge for most of us.

APRIL 2

Gandhi once said, "If all the world practiced an eye for an eye, the world would be filled with blind people." When someone hurts us, our instincts usually tell us to strike back. It feels unnatural not to retaliate, particularly when we see the offender enjoying our hurt.

How do I "turn the other cheek" when the wicked are prospering? ⌣

May I find a way of teaching my heart to let go when my mind has already done so.

APRIL 3

It has been said that the seeds of the Second World War were sown by the peace of the First World War. Making peace is not simply an absence of hostility. We must also look at whether any peace we negotiate addresses the underlying conditions that ignited the conflagration in the first place. And it helps if, when we are victors, we can empathize with the losers, and ask: "Is this a peace that I could live with?"

When I end a spat or a feud with someone, am I doing it in a way that is going to lead to reconciliation, or am I just setting the stage for another argument at a future time? ~

Let me work for the true peace that will bring healing in all of my relationships.

APRIL 4

One of the most difficult aspects of forgiveness is learning to forgive ourselves. When we have done something that has hurt the ones we love, we carry the guilt with us for months, years, even a lifetime. It has been said that "guilt is the gift that keeps on giving."

What steps can I take to allow others to forgive me, so that I can begin the work of forgiving myself? ∼

Let me learn to forgive myself when I fall short of my best intentions and disappoint others.

APRIL 5

We forgive because we want to get on with our lives and not be held back by our anger, no matter how justified it may be. We take a huge developmental step forward when we recognize that forgiving is done as much for ourselves as for others.

What righteous anger am I holding onto at the current time? ∼

Meditate by counting your breaths. As you breathe out, exhale the anger that is holding you back from forgiving someone.

APRIL 6

*Sometimes the things we find most unforgivable
about others bear an uncanny resemblance to our own
shortcomings.*

What is there about my own personality that keeps me
angry at some friend or family member? ∼

Give me the courage to look inside myself and acknowledge my shame.

If we fail to speak up after we have been hurt, part of our anger comes out of our own frustration at not telling the other person that what he or she said hurt us.

What holds me back from telling that person that what he or she said or did was wrong? ∿

Let me find the courage to stand up when I have been wronged—not to shame the other person, but to maintain my human dignity.

APRIL 8

When we have been hurt by another person and the
offender refuses to acknowledge the wrong (let alone
apologize), even when we bring it up, we have to be
willing to relinquish our anger. If we do nothing with
our own feelings of anger and hurt, or seek to direct
them back at the offender, they will fester, spreading
to other relationships and areas of our life.

To what extent am I willing to let another person keep
me waiting for my revenge? ∼

I will focus on letting go so that I can "kick the dust
from my sandals" and move on with my life.

SOME OF THE STRENGTHS of liberal religion also are its weaknesses. For example, liberal religion tends to focus on human potential, God's goodness, reason, individual freedom of belief, tolerance, and hopefulness. But these classic affirmations do not deal much with life's hard dimensions—with evil brought on by human actions, with suffering and loss. It is almost as if the onward-and-upward spirituality has little to say about the losses we face, the pain and suffering we endure, the times in our lives when bad things happen. No wonder, then, that the most severe critics of liberal religion call this proclivity to overlook suffering and evil the weakest dimension of the liberal faith. Often forgotten are those from our past who underwent suffering beyond what most of us will ever have to face. Think about Rev. John Murray, who lost both his wife and son and was thrown into debtor's prison before coming to America to lose himself. Murray's life story is full of failures and losses and repetitive personal depression. Yet even in such losses—maybe even *because* of them—Murray was able to express a deep faith in Providence.

APRIL 9

"I would gladly have lain me down to die.... Despair
seemed taking up its residence in my bosom.... I
wrung my hands in agony.... 'Tis past and I am gone
forever."

—JOHN MURRAY
(on leaving his mother and siblings behind
in Ireland and leaving for England)

How are living and dying interwoven in my life? ∼

Deeper than despair is a hidden hope. God of my failures, do not let me go. Help me to feel the losses but also the promises of new beginnings.

APRIL 10

"Debts crowded upon me. Demands ... were continually made. ... [My wife's] sickness, her death, ... [dashed] from me the cup of felicity, while expenses accumulated. ... I was taken by a writ, ... and borne to a spunging-house [debtors' prison]. ... I prayed most fervently to Him that ... He would grant me my deliverance from a world, where I could serve neither my God, my neighbor, nor myself."

—JOHN MURRAY

What has been the lowest point in my life? Have I ever thought it would be better not to be alive? ⌒

Giver of Life, you know how hard it is to live when we have suffered losses that seem greater than our hearts can bear. But here, in the midst of despair, let the healing fountains start, that I might once again taste of the waters of life.

APRIL 11

"My heart's desire was to pass through life, unheard,
unseen, unknown to all, as though I ne'er had been."

—JOHN MURRAY
(describing his plan to set sail for
America and there lose himself)

Have I ever run away from life? What shape did my
escape take? ～

O God, I have sometimes wished I never had been born,
never had to travel the harsh roads and valleys of my life,
never had to experience the loss of loved ones and felt
my heart torn out. I have spent time running, never realizing that you were ahead, waiting with open arms to
welcome me home.

APRIL 12

"The succeeding Sunday evening [as I was speaking in Boston]... many stones were violently thrown into the windows.... At length, a rugged stone, weighing about a pound and a half, was forcibly thrown in at the window behind my back; it missed me. Had it sped, as it was aimed, it must have killed me. Lifting it up, and waving it in view of the people, I observed: This argument is solid and weighty, but it is neither rational nor convincing.... Not all the stones in Boston, except they stop my breath, should shut my mouth or arrest my testimony."

—JOHN MURRAY

Have I ever felt threatened because of my faith? ⌣

How often we fail to remember that faith costs more than signing a membership book or pledging money to our religious communities. When the time comes, as it must for those who bear witness to the truth, let me not forget that others have borne the cost before me and others have paid dearly with their lives. O God, let me not turn back or forsake what I know to be true in my heart.

APRIL 13

There is not a single person who has never suffered loss or felt despair about living or wondered how to find the strength to go on. If we truly understood this, we might find compassion for others as well as for ourselves, for each of us is fragile and in need of solace.

Who needs my understanding and support today? ~

Teach me to feel compassion for all those who suffer—most especially those closest to me—and help me to respond, not with words alone, but with kind and generous acts.

APRIL 14

Light a candle and stay in silence, remembering your suffering, the suffering of those you love, and the suffering of the whole world, without exception.

What do I hear or sense in the silence? ∽

Suffering Love, which holds my fragile life and the life of the whole planet in your hands, help me to listen and care for others, most especially myself.

APRIL 15

"Be of good cheer, your God is with you, He will never leave you, nor forsake you; He is in the wide waste, as in the full city"

—JOHN MURRAY
(the words he heard within as he thought about coming to America)

What brings me hope and sustains me? ⌒

O God, you are with me always, even 'til the end of time. If love be stronger than death, then what is there to fear?

PRUNUS, THE GENUS that includes the plum, produces the first flower of spring. The plum blossoms are hearty and their fragrance sublime. It is said that the gnarled limbs of *Prunus* are a sign of the coming transformation in spring, and so the *Prunus* is revered.

In Korea there is a spiritual tradition expressed through the creation of vases. The *maebyong* vase is designed to hold one sprig of *Prunus*. In this vase, the *Prunus* is studied and becomes to the eye an object for contemplation. Out of the inner realization of its beauty, truth, like the *Prunus*, is finally revealed.

APRIL 16

*"The very best and utmost of attainment in this life is
to remain still and let God act and speak to thee."*

—MEISTER ECKHART

How can a ritual of stillness bring depth to my understanding of life and of God? ⌣

For so long I have pursued the fulfillment of endless
desires. Though I know the first times will be the hard-
est, let me learn to sit quietly and be guided inward by
my breath.

APRIL 17

"Your treasure house is within. It contains all you will ever need."

—HUI HAI

Books, videos, and the Internet promise me knowledge as nothing has before. How can I trust and value what I find within? ∿

"Bread of Heaven, Bread of Heaven, feed me till I want no more."

—WILLIAM WILLIAMS

APRIL 18

"And the Plant will open its stem to the living waters;
it will become an everlasting source [of blessing]."
—PARABLE OF THE TREES, DEAD SEA SCROLLS

What nourishment do I need to strengthen my life? ∼

Source of Life, let me know that I thirst for that which I
can draw from within. Make me ready to receive, again
and again, your life-giving presence.

APRIL 19

"Meditating on the immobile lotus, your mind takes flight like a butterfly and dabbles in blood red poppies and purple heather."

—ERICA JONG

When I listen to my thoughts and pay attention to my feelings, what do I find? ⌣

Praise be to God, who makes the invisible dance within my soul. Let me find there all kinds of things—deep sorrows and deeper joys.

APRIL 20

"The finding of God is the coming to one's own self."
—MEHER BABA

How much of my day is absorbed by endless activity that keeps me from myself? ⌒

Hundreds of daily tasks, annoyances, and pleasures keep me busy. Let me learn to live differently. Let me know amazing things I can call myself.

APRIL 21

"God enters by a private door into every individual."

—RALPH WALDO EMERSON

What door is left open in my life, allowing for something new to enter? ∽

Help me know that it is you, God, who searches for me. Let me welcome and not refuse you, and let nothing obscure your radiance.

APRIL 22

We are all spiritually wounded before we can even name the hurt. Each of us carries within a pervasive sense of sadness, as if we had lost something precious. And we have. But to name and touch our deep wound is to feel connected to the wounds of others.

How have I been wounded spiritually? ∼

Take these wounds of mine, and make them vehicles of healing for others. Take this sadness of mine, and let it discover joy.

Boston's Shawmut Avenue Universalist Church, under the leadership of Rev. George Perin, became a seven-day-a-week church in the 1890s, providing a wide range of services to neighborhood residents in addition to Sunday offerings. The mission of the church was clearly stated as "a union of those who love, in the service of those who suffer," a simple vision with profound implications. The twin Universalist themes of love and service are evident in the mission and life of the Shawmut Avenue Church. An issue of the church newsletter dated September 23, 1897, outlined a series of meetings for small groups throughout the week—options that ranged from free legal services and childcare for working mothers to Bible study and a class on the life of Rev. John Murray.

APRIL 23

Both the brevity and the clarity of the mission of Shawmut Avenue Universalist Church are often lacking in our churches and lives. The busyness that prevails for most of us focuses our attention on to-do lists and schedules. Each of us needs to set aside time to determine what is truly important to us, and then we need to live by that determination.

What is the mission of my church? What is my mission in life? ∿

Spirit of Life, always growing and always open to us if we will listen, help me to remember who I am, why I am here, and what I can do to help others, so that my time and energy are directed toward what really matters—care of my soul and love and service to others.

APRIL 24

"We are not alone. There is always an unseen power working for our righteousness. The Infinite is behind us. The eternal years of God are ours."

—OLYMPIA BROWN

To whom or what am I committed? ∽

God, power beyond language, unseen but perceived when I dare to feel the energy of the Infinite touching me, help me to feel those moments in my life when I have touched eternity in time and been connected to creation no less than stars or flowers or atoms. Let me stay in silence and remember.

APRIL 25

Flimsy grace and callused hands are all that keep the world in place, keep me in place, keep any of us in place. For the ordinary sacraments of our lives and the lives of all those we love and all those we shall never know, revelation continues.

What do "callused hands" have to do with grace? ⌒

Stifle the rehearsed response, the practiced prayer, the conditional piety, the acts of mercy done for the approval of others. Let me live as I pray and pray as I live.

APRIL 26

"The church exists by mission, as fire exists by burning."
—EMIL BRUNNER

What is the real mission of my spiritual community? 〰

Let me discover the passion of mission in the midst of my community. If it burns brightly, let me follow it; if it burns only a little, let me help to rekindle it.

APRIL 27

"The dodo flies backward because he doesn't care to see where he's going, but wants to see where he's been."

—FRED ALLEN

Do I sometimes worship the past without letting the future emerge? ∼

Spirit of the Future, present now but often unnoticed, wake me up to your potential, that I might have the courage to change.

APRIL 28

How we live our lives—what Ballou saw as "practical Christianity"—speaks as loud as what we say we believe, if not louder.

How does my life reflect my deepest values? ∿

Inner Teacher, let me face my life in terms of my values and seek to bring how I behave in closer harmony with how I wish to behave.

APRIL 29

"What does the Lord require of thee, but to do justly,
and to love mercy, and to walk humbly with thy God?"

—MICAH 6:8

What does God (or my deepest commitment) require me
to do and love and live by? ⌐∽

Holy Spirit in me and in all creation, let me remember
what I trust and where my deepest commitment dwells,
so that I may act justly, forgive myself and others, and
remain on the path of life's deepest truths.

THE MANDATE TO LOVE thy neighbor as thyself is a universal ethnic, described in many of the world's religious traditions as the "golden rule" for human interactions. Yet far too often, this rule is lauded but not practiced. Acting neighborly toward others, especially to those we do not like, is a difficult practice that requires of us the ability to overcome the instinct for self-preservation. And yet we are not told to sacrifice ourselves for the sake of our neighbors. Rather we are told to care for our neighbors as we care for ourselves. Healthy self-love is necessary before we can begin to love others.

APRIL 30

"You see, one of the secrets of life is that we are all ministers. We all have the ability to bless one another. It's true. But it is not easy."

—WEBSTER KITCHELL

Like a monarch of old, how might I confer "neighborhood" upon someone near me today? ⌣

Help me to grow to deeper, more mature ways of living as a person of faith and a neighbor to those around me.

MAY 1

Being a good neighbor does not always require conscious acts of kindness. A woman who struggled to make the time to exercise noticed a neighbor—a man known in the area as a great walker—go past her house at about the same time three days in a row. "He must have changed his route," she thought. "I need to get back out there too." Well, the very next morning she did, and there he was plugging right toward her. As they came near each other he smiled a greeting. The woman said, "Your example drew me back out here. Thanks." He was surprised and just as quickly gone. The woman did not even know the man's name, but his example helped "neighbor" her back to health.

In what ways am I "neighbored" by those around me? ∿

May I be mindful today of those who rekindle my own flickering flame.

MAY 2

Roy and his partner had left their noisy, violent inner-city apartment for a row home in a quiet neighborhood a mile away. It all seemed perfect. Except for Jill. Living right next door, it was impossible to ignore her outbursts of rage. Today she was in a door-slamming tirade. Roy lost it. He stormed outside, shouting at her to stop. As his stunned partner and neighbors looked on, he dashed back inside, slamming his door so that the building shook. Back in his own living room, he seethed in frustration. Suddenly a calm descended on him and an inner voice spoke: "Make peace with her." Roy returned to the porch where Jill still stood. Holding out his hand, he said, "I don't want to live like this. Let's be neighbors." Jill was shaky. "You frighten me," she said. Roy replied quietly, "I'm not a bad man. I want to make peace with you." Now tearful, Jill took his hand.

How can I make peace in myself? ⌒

Help me to remember that peace is not the absence of strife; rather, it is a peaceful spirit amidst the storm.

MAY 3

"We should not serve our neighbor as if she were Jesus. We should serve our neighbor because she is Jesus."

—MOTHER THERESA

Who is my neighbor? ∼

Help me to remember that neighboring is ministry. The most important person is the one in front of me.

MAY 4

Our neighborhoods can help nurture us physically as well as emotionally. The plant known as lamb's quarters—a green that some people say is better than spinach or beet greens—grows wild in abundance in many areas. Lamb's quarters can be used fresh or blanched and frozen for later consumption. We rarely think of our urban neighborhoods as Mother Earth, offering bounty right underfoot to feed us, literally. Yet all we need do is seek, gather, and harvest.

What sustenance can I find in my neighborhood? ∿

We have all that we need, closer and in more abundance than we ever imagine. Let me feel today the sustenance of neighborhood.

The vacant urban lot had been an eyesore for years, so inhospitable that even street thugs no longer went there. An elderly man from the next block began to putter in the lot. He removed the trash, cleared away the rocks, and began to till the soil. Curious passersby began to take an interest in his progress, one or two stopping to help. The man's own life grew richer for the folks he met on the lot. By season's end flowers bloomed as the garden struggled to establish itself. The next summer a veritable Garden of Eden fed the neighbors with beauty for the eye and food for the body. A local parson stopped by to admire the lot. "Isn't it marvelous what the Lord has done here?" he rhapsodized to the old man. "Yes," responded the gardener, "but you should have seen it when the Lord was working it alone."

What actions can I perform today that will demonstrate three things I believe strongly? ∼

God of sweat and persistence, inspire me to put my feet and hands where my faith is.

MAY 6

"God is not hiding in a temple. Torah came to tell the inattentive man: 'You are not alone, you live constantly in a Holy neighborhood; Remember, Love thy neighbor-God-as thyself.' We are . . . asked to . . . keep the spark within aflame, and to suffer His light to reflect in our face."

—ABRAHAM JOSHUA HESCHEL

What is it that keeps the spark within me aflame? ⌒

May I be a blessing unto my neighbors, and they unto me.

THOUGH RELIGION is surely what we do with our solitude, as Alfred North Whitehead observed, it is social, too; for the root of the word means "that which binds" us together. A person who is not afraid of solitude is not afraid of sharing that solitude with others, for the shared solitude leads to community. In community, we are solitudes touching, knowing and respecting one another's individuality, but reaching for that which we have in common. Community is a place where individuals are asked to seek that which is shared, even as each one remains unique. A true community does not ask us to give ourselves up to a greater cause, but to bring ourselves to the cause and share. And therein is the true radical nature of forming a community: a process whereby we are introduced to one another as we are.

*There are many forms of communal life, from the
more traditional church to small, informal spiritual
support groups. One interesting communal experience
was that of the Hopedale Community, founded by
Adin Ballou in the mid–nineteenth century near
Milford, Massachusetts. (Hopedale was the
Universalist counterpart to Brook Farm of the
Unitarian Transcendentalists.) Hopedale's precepts
included opposition to violence in any form.*

Where do I find community? ∼

In my solitude, help me to find others who need me as
much as I need them for mutual care and edification,
support and love, challenge and gentle critique.

A tiny organism is born in a salt marsh, the beginning of an ecological system that flows out and back with the tides, changing, reaping, growing, dying, replacing one thing with another as it feeds itself in this magical chain of living things, predictable and miraculous in the same instant.

What gift can I contribute to my community this very instant? ∽

Collective Spirit, make me simple. May I see that the gifts I bring to this world are a piece of the life that is. May I bow my head, sit quietly still, and receive this knowing.

MAY 9

*"But I say unto you which hear, Love your enemies,
do good to them which hate you. Bless them that
curse you, and pray for them which despitefully use
you."*

—LUKE 6:27–28

Can I expand my heart to encompass even those who do
not like me? ⁓

"May those who wish me harm be well. May they be
happy and peaceful. May no harm come to them. May
they be freed from greed, selfishness, and jealousy.
May they be able to face life's problems with patience,
courage, and understanding."

—BUDDHIST INVOCATION

Established in 1841, the Hopedale Community was presided over by Ballou until 1880, reaching its peak of three hundred members in 1856 (with only fourteen members left in 1876). The community never recovered from the departure of two of its chief stockholders in 1856. An experiment in "practical Christianity," this utopian community based itself on what its founders conceived of as the early Christian model.

What causes rifts or conflict in my spiritual community, and how are these dealt with? ∽

Help me to see that conflict may be the occasion for growth and differences may offer the opportunity to see a new direction, so that difficult people become my teachers.

MAY 11

"I hold myself bound . . . never . . . to kill, assault, beat, torture, rob, oppress, persecute, defraud, corrupt, slander, revile, injure, envy or hate any human being— even my worst enemy."

—HOPEDALE COMMUNITY ENTRANCE DECLARATION

What are the promises I made, either explicitly or implicitly, by entering my spiritual community? ～

God, I hold myself bound to be a just and loving person, but you know how often I fall short, how soon I forget my own faults, and how often I remember the faults of others. Help me to look at myself without the need to justify myself and to look at others with more compassion.

MAY 12

*There are many diverse religious and spiritual faiths
and beliefs. To support and witness loving spiritual
practices of different cultures can help to open our
eyes to the richness of spiritual yearning and the deep
flow of spiritual life in the peoples of this earth. To
immerse ourselves in varying types of meditations and
prayers can give us a new perspective on our own
beliefs and traditions.*

Do I find myself hesitant to explore the rich spiritual traditions and practices of other cultures and peoples?
What holds me back? ⌒

Creator of All Life, open my heart to the loving spirit
that flows within many faiths and religious practices.
Allow me to see the miraculous specter of your unending
Being in the kaleidoscope of rich traditions.

William Ellery Channing, an early spokesman for American Unitarianism, respected the Hopedale Community but felt that eventually there would be conflict between individual needs and community needs. This kind of conflict continues today in any faith that puts some focus on individual freedom of belief.

Have I ever suspended my need for individual freedom for the greater good of my spiritual community? If not, are there circumstances in which I might do so? ∽

We are not here to remain apart from others, but to enter into communion with them, just as we are to enter into communion with You, Spirit of Truth. Grant me today a little less of "me" and more of "us," that I might understand how deeply connected I am already to all that is.

L IVING IN HARMONY with nature, asking for no more than what we truly need to survive, is a spiritual discipline few of us practice. Our culture often leads us to believe that luxuries are essential, to purchase what we don't really require, and to prepare for future financial security when none of us can predict the future. If we take time to look around us and listen with our hearts, we will see that the earth itself is sufficient for our needs. The plants and animals know this instinctively.

MAY 14

*Our senses are deadened by the onslaught of the
media—TV, radio, print, and the Internet—and by
the hubbub of city life. When vacations take us into
the wilderness, we can experience what it is to live by
the rhythms of nature. Picture a descending harvest
moon casting golden-orange ripples on the water as it
gives way to the sun. Imagine a blue heron patiently
scouting for fish. Think of goldfinches at the thistle;
jays, chickadees, and nuthatches hunting for seeds;
woodpeckers hammering at the bark; and the eagle—
oh, the bald eagle—flying overhead. As the urban
camper wakes to his first morning in the woods, the
wind picks up, tousles the smooth lake, flutters cot-
tonwood leaves, and sweeps sleepy cobwebs from his
mind. A day begins.*

In what ways can I sense the daily ebb and flow of life
beyond the noise of cars and layers of concrete? ∼

Let me live in harmony with nature's rhythm, and let it
fill me with peace.

A choir of birds is singing, joyous to be alive, lost in their song, shouting a great greeting to a deaf world. We ought not spoil the glories of dawn or the fading light of evening with anxiety or depression or fear. Rather, we should just feel pleasure that we are alive and can hear these birds, who seem to know so much more than we do.

When am I joyful? ∼

Help me to feel joy for the gifts of life, no matter how small they may seem, so that gratitude may fill my heart and help my soul to sing.

MAY 16

Even when we immerse ourselves in nature, we some-
times fail to notice our surroundings. If we race
around the lake in a speedboat or become obsessed
with catching a record-breaking fish, we may not see
a blue heron in the reeds, a pair of loons outfishing
us, a bald eagle flapping across the lake, a muskrat
paddling by with only its head showing. We need to
take time to "pick more daisies."

What do I miss in my rush to get to a distant shore? ⌇

On my daily journeys let there be a stillness within and
time to drink deeply from the wellspring of beauty.

In some lakeshore areas, a plant known as purple loose strife is taking over, multiplying as quickly as kudzu. With beautiful purple flowers on a stalk, this plant is lovely, yet it chokes out other shoreline vegetation. Some jurisdictions plagued by this plant are introducing insects that consume it. In four years the insects should restore equilibrium.

But that's a misnomer, for there is never true equilibrium, only a seesaw adjustment to more or less—so much like our lives. We long for an impossible balance, adjusting to the too-muches and too-littles, flailing at ourselves for being unable to bring this about. How much better to accept these fluctuations, adjusting to them, knowing that our bodies, our lives naturally are drawn toward homeostasis.

If I have done what I can do, can I let go of my worries today? ∽

Spirit of Peace, help me to be patient in my struggle for balance and have faith that I naturally lean into that calm center.

MAY 18

Deepak Chopra talks about times when everything
slows down, even our aging process. We have all had
moments like these, and they are to be treasured.
Perhaps good friends huddle under a moth-eaten
blanket and a vast, starry sky, counting falling stars
and singing in voices soft as lapping waves. For those
friends, reality rests and time stretches its wings.

On what occasions has the passage of time become
unimportant to me? What meaning did this have for
me? ∼

Let me cherish those times when I am completely in the
present. They are holy moments.

Loons have a lot to teach us about living. Unperturbed, relaxed, they go about their business, occasionally upending for a two-minute dive, then popping back to the surface with their prize. We yearn to grease through the water like loons, knowing what our life is about, diving for sustenance, calling to our mates. Loons are lodestones, slowing us down, drawing us to the uncomplicated life. There's something so beautiful in a routine, skeletal in construction. It's simple stuff, and sometimes we need to live simply.

In what ways have I made my daily routine a calming experience? What more could I do? ⌒

Let me find the quiet composure of the loon in each day. Let me swim peacefully in the water, cutting clean through the waves.

Albert Schweitzer said, "I am the life that wills to live in the midst of life that wills to live." We are all part of that life stream that flows into our being. We are part of the breath of waves that calms our spirits. This is especially clear when we listen to the night voices: tree frogs answering back and forth, bullfrogs garumping, distant highway cars, fish slapping the water, muskrats splashing as they gather food. As we listen to our own contributions—yawning, the clinking of dishes, the rustling of bedclothes—we can feel that we too are a part of this night symphony.

What connections have I found to the greater world? ∼

Help me to remember that all life is one, connected by a blazing energy pulsating with love.

IN THE LIBERAL church tradition, what binds people into religious community is the covenants they freely make with one another. A covenant can be said to be the ultimate promise people make to one another in the light of the heritage and mission of the church.

For many generations, both Universalist and Unitarian covenants were overtly Christian, although most contained so-called "freedom clauses" that safeguarded individual freedom of belief. Hence, many covenants begin with such words as "we unite" or "we affirm" rather than "we believe," making the covenants relational, not doctrinal. More recent covenants, such as the Unitarian Universalist covenant adopted as a bylaw of the 1984 and 1985 General Assemblies (and since updated), are intentionally pluralistic in religious orientation.

Covenants are whole or come alive when there is a degree of consistency between what people profess to hold true and how they live in community and in the wider world. They are broken—promises made and not kept—when there is a distance between what people profess to believe and how they act. Breaches in covenant are felt in the midst of community life, but they are not always acknowledged. In fact, many discrepancies between values and behaviors are denied, and for many such discrepancies the community provides no way for people to seek forgiveness or to atone.

MAY 21

Two of the areas that seem especially to lead to broken covenants are those of class and race. If every person is important and justice is a value, as we so often state, why do so many communities seem class or racially segregated? As many have commented, the great American dream (or covenant) will never be realized until racism and classism are confronted.

How much personal contact do I have with people of color in my present religious community? ∼

God, if we truly affirm that you see all of us as your children, help me to build a beloved community in which all may enter. Let me live as I say I covenant, that the human family may be reunited.

MAY 22

"In 1968 when black involvement in the denomination was at a high point, blacks numbered 1,500 of the denomination's 180,000 members, less than one percent."

—UNITARIAN UNIVERSALIST REGISTER-LEADER,
May 1968

How prominent are people of color in my spiritual community? ∼

Help me to look inside and see what it is that separates me from others, and then to be someone who lives what I profess.

MAY 23

Dr. Martin Luther King, Jr. often preached that Sunday morning at 11 A.M. was the most segregated hour in America. Why does this chasm still exist if we know in our hearts that we want to be more inclusive and that we are divided against ourselves when we separate into pockets of racial or economic sameness?

How can I help my spiritual community become more inclusive? ～

For shortness of vision, fear of speaking out, hardness of heart, and unwillingness to ask for others what I know to be good for myself, I ask forgiveness and the courage to be a prophet.

"We believe it to be inconsistent with the notion of the human race in a common Saviour, and the obligations to mutual love, which flow from that union, to hold any part of our fellow creatures in bondage. We, therefore, recommend a total refraining from the African trade and the adoption of prudent measures for the gradual abolition of the slavery of the negroes in our country, and for the instruction and education of their children in English literature, and in the principles of the Gospel."

—1790 PHILADELPHIA CONVENTION OF UNIVERSALISTS

What have I done to combat racism in ways that cost something personally? ∿

I believe that every human being has worth and every person is a child of God. Help me to act on these two abiding principles of faith in my life and in my community.

MAY 25

"We covenant to affirm and promote the inherent worth and dignity of every person."

—UNITARIAN UNIVERSALIST STATEMENT OF PRINCIPLES AND PURPOSES, 1984–1985

In what respect is the covenant broken for me and for my religious community? ∿

Knowing that I have fallen short of my deepest values, I ask for the strength to deepen my faith and increase my understanding, so that I might become a whole person in a broken world.

MAY 26

"No prominent Universalist layman is known to have been associated with any anti-slavery organization outside the denomination after 1830."

—RUSSELL MILLER

How deeply is racism woven into the fabric of my faith and the structure of my spiritual community? ∽

God, I need to begin somewhere. Let that beginning start with me but not end there. Let me be an instrument of your benevolence toward all creation, so that your inclusive love may draw me and others into a kingdom of mutual respect.

We gather in community to seek unity of spirit in the midst of diversity, to heal the wounded and confront the oppressor, to instill joy and confidence in our children, to grow in mind, body, heart, and spirit, and to bear witness to the transforming power of love beyond which not a single atom nor person is lost forever. Thus do we covenant with each other in the presence of that which is holy and universal.

What is one specific action I or my religious community might take to combat racism? ⁓

O God, in the end it won't matter how much I have, but how much I have given. It won't matter how much I know, but rather how much I love. And it won't matter how much I say I don't believe, but rather how deeply I live the truths I say I do believe.

ACH DAY is a precious gift. Each day is a new beginning. What is "holy" is what appears to be most "ordinary"—everyday existence. Sometimes we can recognize this truth on good days; on more difficult days, it is a truth we may have a hard time feeling in our hearts. Sometimes during difficult times, a listening ear or helping hand can make all the difference, reminding us that none of us is alone. Oscar Wilde once wrote, "We are all in the gutter, but some of us are looking at the stars." Looking at the stars is the best way of thanking God for the un-earned gifts we receive day after day.

MAY 28

One of the affirmations from a Bernie Siegel video says, "Accept the gift of each day." When we are depressed or sick, it's difficult to see the beauty of a day as a gift, much less open the package. But those gifts are there all the same, appearing in the strangest places and seemingly incidental.

Can I find something in each day that I feel is a gift given to me unannounced? ∼

Let me be open to the gifts, messages, and comfort of each day, for they are waiting for me. They are lights that shine within me and through me, making me smile.

MAY 29

"There is that near you which will guide you,
Oh, wait for it.
And be sure that ye keep to it."

—ISAAC PENINGTON

Do I believe that there are no coincidences? ∼

As I evolve through the steps of fear, depression, and anger, let me remember that I can meet the Buddha at any time and be healed.

MAY 30

In the darkest depths of a night filled with worrisome dreams, sometimes we feel like giving up. There is a story of a faith healer who ran a filling station. A family with a child who was seriously ill with cancer stopped for gas. While the parents were looking elsewhere, the healer put her arms around the child, hugged him gently, and whispered that he would be all right.

Can I be patient and have faith that help will come? ∼

In the midst of despair, let me be still and know that I am surrounded by love; let me believe that there is no stronger Power than love and I am loved.

MAY 31

Every day's a fortune cookie, says my California friend (perhaps because she's been eating Chinese food for lunch for months). Every day has a fortune cookie waiting for us if only we try to find it. A cancer patient was getting progressively unhappier about her second chemotherapy cycle, which was coming soon. While taking a shower, she suddenly "saw" the shampoo packet that had been there for months on the window sill. This time the words jumped out: "Infusium 23—Creates, Restores, Structurizes." Of course! That's exactly what the chemo was doing.

What are some fortuitous messages that have spoken to me? ∼

Let my mind be open to seeing things from a different perspective—one that is healing and restorative.

JUNE 1

Losing hair due to illness or age is not the end of the world, but it is somewhat disconcerting, especially when it comes out in clumps. Anne Morrow Lindbergh cut her son Reeve's hair once a year before summer camp and threw the clippings out for the birds. What a great idea.

What are other ways to view my difficult experiences? 〜

May I accept the changes that come, use them creatively, and turn them into joy.

JUNE 2

Think of the gifts—a gentle word of understanding, a ride to the airport, a meal, a massage—that have come to you at a special time. The smallest of thoughtful acts can make the difference.

What gift of kindness or thoughtfulness has made a difference for me? ⌢

Let me give gifts from the heart, gifts of love.

JUNE 3

Each day brings a special gift—a friend calls, a child laughs, the sun shines or the rains fall, the leaves change color, music fills the air, a train whistles in the distance. Each day can be a joyful day.

What is my list of joys today? ~

In the most ordinary of days the sunlight sparkles in my heart.

"LET US JOIN together in silent prayer and meditation." When we hear these words in worship, we rarely have time to do more than shut our eyes before the minister says, "Amen." If the silence approaches sixty seconds, people squirm in the pews.

The unprogrammed worship of the Quakers offers food for the spirit and strength for living. This worship includes a period of silent prayer and meditation, a time for listening to "the voice of God within." It takes a lot of practice to sort through the clutter in our minds and spirits, but there is no more powerful act than settling into silence and truly *listening*.

We are each alone, but in silence we are not lonely. In the heart of our solitude, if we listen with our hearts, there is One who dwells with us, calling out to us, though we seldom listen. By learning how to stay with silent prayer and expectation, we practice the presence of God. If we experience prayer as encountering God— approaching God as a forgiving and loving Presence, but also as the One who helps us see our own short-comings and fears—we grow spiritually. Prayer is not just about feeling good, but also about feeling guilt and fear and pain—and being strengthened in the process.

So here is a gift for this week. Settle into silence and solitude every day for five minutes. Find a place where you can spend that time uninterrupted. Where that place is or when is up to you.

JUNE 4

Sometimes we all need to sit in silent prayer and medi-
tation until we feel ourselves drawn within, comforted,
nestled in the arms of a quiet presence, nurtured by
a motherly stroke.

When I sit in prayer or meditation, do I feel my mind
wandering, thinking about thinking, concerned about an
issue from my day, unfocused? ∼

Let my restless heart slow down, be patient, take time to
restore itself.

JUNE 5

"Speech is of time; silence is of eternity."

—THOMAS CARLYLE

In my silence, have I felt the presence of that which is beyond, yet within, time itself? 〜

Eternal One who rests in silence, help me to listen to your voice, though it be sometimes as whispers in the wind or, other times, as cries in the night.

JUNE 6

"The world would be happier if men had the same capacity to be silent that they have to speak."

—BARUCH SPINOZA

Can I keep silent without feeling awkward? ∽

In the midst of a noisy world, help me to stay still and hear my heart beating.

JUNE 7

"Silence is one great art of conversation."

—WILLIAM HAZLITT

How can silence speak? ～

Out of the depths have I spoken to the universe, yet often heard nothing but the tone and sound of my own voice. Teach me how to listen more carefully to that which is not my own voice, but the voice of someone speaking within.

JUNE 8

Silence can be profoundly active, as when Jesus refused to speak to Pilate, who asked him if he was the son of God. Silence can also be deadly, as when people refuse to speak out in the face of injustice.

When was the last time I failed to speak out in the face of injustice? ∼

Help me to keep silent when my words would only be misused, but help me to speak clearly when I see others being treated unkindly or injustice being perpetrated.

JUNE 9

Settling into silence can center us and bring calm clarity. When we settle into solitude, we let it touch our souls and bring peace.

Can I touch and feel my calm center? ∼

In the clearness of my heart, teach me the meaning of peace, for myself and for others.

JUNE 10

In the sanctuary of silence, we are surrounded with that clarity of mind and heart that allows us to walk without fear.

When have I felt fearless? ∽

Be still and practice the presence of God.

PRAYER IS LOVE in action. To practice prayer, therefore, we must make an effort to be open to ourselves and others and to listen without judging. To give love, we must first love ourselves. To love ourselves, we must accept ourselves, faults and all. To receive love, we must feel ourselves worthy of it. We all have moments of doubt when we are not sure we deserve to give or receive love. When love makes its way past the obstacle of self-doubt, it is all the more wonderful. Wrapped in the arms of loving, we understand the mystery of being human.

JUNE 11

Giving and receiving love is the basis of our being fully human. To be whole one must both give and accept love.

How often do I feel loved? ∽

Lover of Creation, help me to accept love from others simply because I am a person of worth.

JUNE 12

Most of us know what it is like to waver on a decision about whether or not to rise to a challenge when we have just an inkling of faith in ourselves. More often than not we back away, unwilling to risk failure. Sometimes, though, we are blessed by someone who comes along and enthusiastically encourages us to stretch our wings and fly. That encouragement can make all the difference.

Can I open my heart and become a person who encourages others to take on worthy missions and challenges? ∼

Lord, help me pay attention and listen to those around me. Help me inspire others to grow in ways that stretch the mind, body, and soul.

JUNE 13

When we plant the seeds of love, we never know what might come of that love. A woman fed the birds in a birdfeeder near her house, taking care to keep the feeder full as new families of birds flocked to the yard. As the summer ripened, the woman noticed large, bright sunflowers growing along the hedgerow of her lane. The birds had planted a surprise garden of sunflowers from the food she had left them.

Am I ever stingy with myself and my gifts, holding back the love that I have to share? ⌣

Center of Life, unfold before me the truth that the more I give of myself, the more I will behold the Great Creation reflecting back on me the generous, abundant miracle of life.

Sometimes we repeat our mistakes and need to learn the same lesson over and over again. When we correct our course and it does not hold, we may be holding onto old beliefs or routines that we are reluctant to change, and when we learn this lesson we may be opened to new lessons at a higher level of consciousness. By letting go of a bad habit, we may have more time to be creative and productive. When we face this challenge, we need to love ourselves and be gentle with our "blind spots." These recurring challenges happen for a reason, and when we truly get beyond a hurdle, we appreciate ourselves for it all the more for the discipline it took to achieve the goal.

Do I criticize myself harshly over a lesson I cannot seem to learn? ∽

Great God of Wisdom, help me be gentle with myself as I learn to follow a healthy path on my earthly journey. As you reveal my "blind spots" to me, help me to acknowledge my human limitations and accept that there will always be something new to learn.

JUNE 15

Many people have wonderful relationships with animals. Some of us love to watch and feed birds as they stop in our yards. Some of us own cherished pets—dogs, cats, horses—who are nothing short of full members of the family. Some of us care for animals in zoos, animal hospitals, humane societies, or on farms. Some of us love to study or watch wild creatures in their natural habitats, such as moose, elk, elephants, or tigers. We are part of the animal kingdom, and we have a special role to play as caretakers.

Have I considered my role in my relationship with all of God's creatures? ⌒

Lord of All Being, guide me in compassion as I live with and am surrounded by the multitude of creatures with whom I share this earthly life. Help me to see that as a member of your earthly community, I am blessed with the ability to enjoy, nurture, and even heal these other creatures. Help me to see this as a blessed responsibility in my walk through life.

JUNE 16

We are called to help people who face their own death or the death of a loved one. We can help by soothing others, especially children, when a loved one has died. We can attend to the passing of souls, and to those who grieve their passing. We must remember that the loss of a loved one is felt as deeply by a child as by an adult. The child needs to hear the truth about the situation, within the loving and supportive care of the adults in the family and the community.

Do I take the time to be present with those who are grieving when they need me? ⌣

Great Spirit, help me acknowledge that there is nothing more important than my complete presence with and for those who have lost loved ones. Help me attend to them with gentleness, patience, and care.

JUNE 17

"For I was an hungred, and ye gave me meat: I was thirsty, and ye gave me drink: I was a stranger, and ye took me in. Naked, and ye clothed me: I was sick, and ye visited me: I was in prison, and ye came unto me.... Inasmuch as ye have done it unto one of the least of these my brethren, ye have done it unto me."

—MATTHEW 25:35, 36, 40

Am I able to see the Divine in each person? ∽

I pray for the happiness, peace, and safety of all people. May we all face our lives with patience, courage, and understanding.

L IVING A prayerful life means learning how to accept losses as well as successes, changes as well as stability, pain as well as joy. We tend to think of spirituality as a joyful experience only, but mystics of all traditions know the "dark night of the soul" and embrace it for what it may teach. For the simple fact is that we learn as much from our failures as from our successes, from having to let go as from holding on. It is in the struggle that we sometimes discover truth, in the presence of suffering that we see goodness, in difficulties that we find meaning.

JUNE 18

Too often we spend time and energy focusing on what is wrong with us or others, with worries about our health or finances, with that which upsets us. For today, spend time remembering what is good about your life.

What is good about my life? ∼

In blessed silence, I draw what is good about my life into a circle of love, where neither time nor space may take them from me again.

JUNE 19

When asked to summarize his philosophy, Plato reportedly said: Practice dying. Living and dying are not opposite but complementary. There always is death in the midst of life, and life out of death. The courage to live is found in accepting death as part of life and in making one's life worth the living.

What is it about death that frightens me? ∼

Dear Comforter, help me to feel the words of Psalm Twenty-Three: "Yea, though I walk through the valley of the shadow of death, I will fear no evil, for thou art with me."

JUNE 20

*"Behold, I make all things new. . . . I am Alpha and
Omega, the beginning and the end."*

—REVELATION 21:5–6

Is there anything really new in all creation? ⌣

O God, help me to accept change as part of living, yet
keep me close to the ground on which I walk, rooted and
centered, so that during all life's transitions something
still and quiet remains within.

JUNE 21

No one is perfect. Each one of us has shortcomings. The art of living is not in denying one's own short-comings, but in realizing them and learning how to grow.

What are my major shortcomings? ～

Let me not pray that I am *un*like other people, but that I am terribly *like* them. Help me see that often those I like the least are there as teachers to show me my own shortcomings. Rid me of selfhood that seeks only to pro-mote itself, and let me learn how to forgive myself and others.

JUNE 22

Today remember Jesus, the prophet. Remember Jesus, who taught the nearness of God in the presence of the ordinary. Remember Jesus, who stormed the castles of the orthodox and spoke truth. Remember Jesus, who was never successful by the world's standards, but surrounded himself with outcasts. Remember Jesus, who needed solitude and responded to Pilate's question about truth with silence. Remember Jesus, who was abandoned by his friends.

What has not being successful taught me? ∼

God, you seem far away and sometimes unconcerned with my troubles. But let me seek you in silence and in others, in nature and in prayer, in sacred books and holy people, in my inner sanctuary and in acts of compassion.

JUNE 23

Spirit *means "life"; thus* spiritual *means having to do with life, hopefully with its depth. Like Jacob in the Jewish scriptures, who is reported to have wrestled with God and refused to let go, we too have wrestled with life, and sometimes without victory. However difficult it may be for us to understand, we must learn that surrender to life is also a way of recovery and restoration. Sometimes we need to let go before we can move on.*

What life issues do I need to let go of so that I can move on? ∼

Let me let go of that which holds me back from life and move on, so that I might be a whole person in a broken world.

JUNE 24

Whenever we wonder why there is something and not nothing; whenever we step outside our needs to be with someone else in their pain; whenever we open our eyes to spend time observing one small flower; whenever in silence we feel at one with everything—in these brief moments the veil is lifted for us and we can see out the windows of time into the open spaces. In those moments we know what it is to be unafraid.

When, if ever, has "the veil been lifted" for me? What was the experience like? ∼

Help and keep me connected to what brings me deeper hope, that I may not be afraid, knowing that love is stronger than death.

EVERY HUMAN BEING faces obstacles, adversity, difficult situations. Learning how to live is learning how to accept what cannot be changed, but it is also learning to change what must be changed. Times of adversity often teach us about strengths we did not know we had. When life seems easy, we are not called to draw on the inner resources we require during hard times. And when we find these resources, we grow. We learn our capabilities; our fear of the unknown diminishes. We develop trust in a force larger than ourselves that sometimes carries us into unknown territory and sees us safely through to the other side. It is often only in retrospect that we see struggle as the soul's education.

JUNE 25

In The Poetics, *Aristotle tells us that the highest form of literature is tragedy. None of us is perfect, and sometimes we get ourselves into situations because of our "tragic flaws." When we overcome those flaws and go on to accomplishment, success is that much sweeter.*

What situations lead me down the wrong path most easily? ⌣

Let me have the wisdom to recognize my limitations and move beyond them.

JUNE 26

Vaclav Havel tells us that hope is most important when our chances for success are the least likely.

What challenges that I am facing appear to be insurmountable? ⌢

Let me have the courage to see my way through adversity, even when hope is most distant.

JUNE 27

*In sports, on a given day either team can win. That's
why games are played in the first place; if the outcome were certain, no one would compete. The most
exciting games to watch are the ones in which the
underdog rallies to win. It is a case of the unexpected
exceeding our expectations. That is why everyone
cheers for David against Goliath.*

At what times in my life have I overcome expectations
and accomplished the unexpected? ∼

Help me to reach within myself to find the courage and
strength to overcome my fears.

JUNE 28

Though the media make much of our sports heroes,
not all great athletes are recognized as such. Consider
the man who, after a serious accident, had been
through surgery and was now going through painful
physical therapy, rebuilding his muscles so that he
could walk again. One day he and his roommate
watched a baseball game together in their hospital
room. The announcers threw around superlatives as
they described the "great players" on the "great team."
Yet who was the greater athlete: the MVP in that
game, or the hospitalized spectator dedicated to a dif-
ficult recovery?

What has it been like to pick myself up from the prover-
bial floor? ⌇

Let me look up and not be afraid to lift myself up when
I bottom out.

JUNE 29

We use the term "survivor" to refer both to those who survived the Holocaust and to those who have lost someone to suicide. Both types of survivors have suffered profound losses. Indeed, perhaps the most important people in their lives have been taken away from them. It is ironic that the same term is used for both types of loss. It suggests that the real meaning of survivor is "the one who has no choice but to go on living."

What are the most significant losses that I have suffered in my life? ∼

I give thanks for the resilience of the human spirit.

JUNE 30

Albert Camus taught us that life is absurd. We can either live with the absurdity, or we can kill ourselves. There are times when each of us is treated unfairly for no just cause. At those times, we can either give in or we can find a reason for living—even if life seems absurd.

How can I replenish the well within myself that sustains me when it seems that there is no good reason to stand up for myself? ∿

May I always see my innate worth and dignity, even when others, including those whom I love and care about, would take it away.

JULY 1

As a child, Glenn Cunningham was badly burned in a fire and lost several toes. He grew up during the Great Depression, when every penny counted. He would run errands for neighbors to earn money. By the time he graduated from college, he ran the fastest mile in America.

How have I used my wounds to become even stronger than before? ∽

Let me look at my wounds as opportunities to make myself a better person.

PARABLES ARE CENTRAL to the life and teachings of Jesus. They are stories that lead us to reach our own conclusions about what is central to a moral and responsible life. Parables do not tell us what to believe, but they provide concrete examples to which we can relate. They show us abstract principles played out in terms of human motivations, emotions, and consequences that we can recognize as common to us all. More often than not, parables confront us with life issues we'd rather not face. Parables are akin to revelations in that we are drawn into the stories before we know it, only to discover ourselves there. Then our minds are awakened and our hearts stirred.

JULY 2

If we are truly awake to the present moment, no life events are either trivial or ordinary. The commonplace opens windows to deeper truths, universes of meaning usually missed.

What kind of a story am I now in (a comedy, a tragedy, an adventure, ...)? ⌣

Help me to see my story as connected to all other stories, and my struggles and joys as the struggles and joys of every person, yet at the same time, unique.

JULY 3

A city dweller decided to plant a small garden in the space behind her house. Some seeds fell on the pavement and birds came and ate them. Other seeds fell in shallow soil where the roots could not take hold. Still other seeds fell among dandelions and never grew to become flowers. But some of the seeds fell on good earth and grew into great sunflowers that rose to touch the tops of kitchen windows so that the city dweller could greet each day in beauty.

Where is my "good earth"? ～

God of Good Soil, help me to plant so that you might sow gentleness and respect and love among all your children.

JULY 4

The kingdom of mutual respect is akin to a mustard seed that is taken and planted in a field. The mustard seed seems the least of all plants, but when grown it is the greatest, because it becomes a large bush in whose branches birds come and rest.

Have I ever watched as a small, seemingly insignificant act of kindness rippled and grew to touch others? ⌒

Let me show compassion to others, as I would hope they would show compassion to me.

JULY 5

A person making a cross-country trip stopped by the side of the highway to take a break. While stretching her legs, she saw a street person lying hurt under an overpass. The man had apparently been mugged and left where he'd fallen. The traveler got into her car and drove away fast, fearful for her own life. A pastor saw the street person, too, and even slowed down to take a closer look, but seeing that the man was bruised and somewhat bloodied, the pastor drove by, making a mental note to check on whether his liability insurance covered him when assisting strangers. A third woman, driving an old model car with four children in the back seat, stopped on the shoulder and knelt down by the street person. She had little extra money but decided she simply couldn't leave him there, so she got her children to help lift him into the car and took him to a local hospital. After his wounds had been treated, she took him to a YMCA, where she secured a room for him for the night. The next morning, she went back to make sure he was alright.

Why do some writers say that "strangers are angels in disguise"? ⌣

God, I am like other people. Help me to remember that truth and act on it.

JULY 6

There was a man who had everything he wanted—a large new home in the best part of the city, money to waste, and employees to do his work while he lived off the company he had founded. He spent the better part of his life doing exactly what he wanted to make himself happy, taking long trips to Europe and giving away funds to local charities. By all outward signs, he was successful. But early one morning he had a heart attack, and as he grabbed his chest in pain, he heard a small voice within looking for his soul.

What is worth more than my life? ⌇

May I hear within me the inner voice that values my soul above all possessions.

JULY 7

There was a judge in the suburbs who cared for neither the law nor people and a woman who kept hounding him for justice. Finally, the judge gave in to her demands because he was afraid that, if he didn't, the woman would go to the newspapers.

What injustice nags at me and won't let go? ⁓

Judge of my heart, let me hear the cries for justice all around me and not be deaf.

JULY 8

*The people were fighting over who was in control of
the congregation. They called in conflict mediators
and outside officials, but the fighting continued.
Finally, one of their most respected leaders could take
it no more. She went downstairs and brought up a
small child from the religious education program.
Placing the child in their midst, she said, "This is why
we're here. Stop your bickering."*

How do I deal with conflict? ⁓

O child in our midst, teach me the meaning of what is
most important.

WHEN WE ACT with compassion toward others, we stop being separate from others and enter into union with them, opening ourselves to a richer experience of life. To feel compassion is to suffer with someone. When we help others, we help ourselves as well, because each one of us is connected and all pain is universal. In some congregations, the service begins with these words: "There are no strangers here, only friends who have not met." If we could truly feel this in our hearts and act on it as an ethical principle, our communities would become sanctuaries of friendship, communities of strangers connected by shared experiences.

JULY 9

Abbott John Daido Loori of the Mountains and Rivers Order of Zen Buddhism spoke of compassion in a dharma discourse: "Compassion is not the same as doing good, or being nice. Compassion functions freely, with no hesitation, no limitation. It happens with no effort, the way you grow your hair, the way your heart beats, the way your blood circulates, or the way you do the ten thousand other things you do moment to moment. It does not take any conscious effort. Someone falls, you pick them up. There is no separation."

Have I ever reached out to help someone as a natural impulse, without thinking, because it was the right thing to do? ⌒

May I empty myself so I may see all that is about me with an open heart. Help me to move in heartful action that I may learn, again and again, that I am not separate but part of the great Oneness of all things.

JULY 10

"The Lord is gracious and full of compassion; slow to anger, and of great mercy."

—PSALM 145:8

Where in my daily life do I experience the steadfast love and compassion of the Sacred? ∽

O Adonai, Lord, O Sacred Source, may I find your healing love present to me in all my days. May I feel your steadfastness amid the swirl of these times. O Sacred Compassion, may you extend out through me to all the world.

JULY 11

So much in our world is limited by conditions and boundaries. Acts of compassion move us into the realm of the unconditional and unbounded, for no other reason than that the source of compassion resides in unconditional, unbounded love.

When acting from my compassion, am I ever able to glimpse (or imagine) a realm of unconditional love? What does that realm look like? ∿

May I move for just an instant beyond my world of consensus limits and self-imposed boundaries to glimpse a world of infinite love.

JULY 12

*"The likeness of those who extend their wealth in the
way of God is as the likeness of a grain of corn that
sprouts seven ears, in every ear a hundred grains. So
God multiplies unto whom He will; God is All-
embracing, All-knowing. Those who expend their
wealth in the way of God . . . their wage is with their
Lord, and no fear shall be with them, neither shall
they sorrow."*

—KORAN

What is my wealth that I may give away? ∿

May I give what I possess without thought of reward,
without reproach for its use. May I give freely that I may
forgive and remember only love.

JULY 13

The three virtues of Hinduism are called the three da's: damyata (self-restraint), datta (giving), and dayadhvam (compassion). The Brhadaranyaka Upanishad *says, "This same thing does the divine voice thunder: Da! Da! Da!"*

Can I recall a time when I or someone I know showed self-restraint, felt called to give, and revealed compassion through the giving? ∿

The Divine Voice thunders self-restraint, giving, compassion. May I stand in awe before the universe—the giver of abundance—which bequeaths to me compassionate life.

JULY 14

Meister Eckhart wrote, "Compassion divinely adorns the soul, clothing it in the robe which is proper to God."

At a time when I unreservedly helped someone, did I find myself transported from the realm of self-concern to a broader awareness of self and others? If I have not had that experience, can I imagine such a time? ⌒

May my actions arise only from love. May I cast off this husk of self-absorption and clothe my innermost being in the sacred light of compassion.

JULY 15

"The whole idea of compassion is based on a keen
awareness of the interdependency of all these living
beings, which are all part of one another and all
involved in one another."

—THOMAS MERTON

When I act from my compassionate heart, am I aware of
my inseparable interdependence with the web of life? ⁓

May I act from my compassion born of the awareness of
my oneness with all, and may my acts of compassion
show me, again and again, that we are all held and
healed in that Oneness.

IN A SEMINARY CLASS on racism in church and society, one white participant was suddenly overcome by the enormity of the evil—the destructive, pervasive erosion of visible and invisible racism. She blurted out, "What can *I* possibly bring to this conversation?" A classmate, an African-American woman in a predominantly white denomination, responded quietly, "Until white people learn to acknowledge and name their own pain of oppression, they will remain 'the Brute.'"

JULY 16

Sometimes we distance ourselves from feeling the pain of others who are oppressed. Yet, our wholeness may depend on getting outside our comfort zones in order to grow.

What pain have I experienced as a result of injustice due to my own racism, classism, or prejudices regarding gender, faith, or ability? ⌒

Please, God, help me to acknowledge the prejudices that are lodged in my heart so that my actions reflect only the principles I profess.

JULY 17

Many of us have no significant relationships with individuals different from ourselves. "I'm not racist," we say. "I just don't know any blacks [Hindus, Latinos, persons with disabilities, you name it]." But that's not the end of the issue. We need to ask ourselves, "Why not?"

In what way can I open my ears and eyes and heart to a deeper relationship with "Another" in my community? ∽

"Open mine eyes that I may see
Visions of truth thou hast for me
Open mine eyes, Illuminate me
Spirit Divine."

—CLARA H. SCOTT

JULY 18

Sometimes our best lessons in generosity come when we are the recipients. When a congregation in York, Pennsylvania, needed a temporary home, they decided to approach Crispus Attucks Community Center two blocks away. Founded in the 1930s to provide recreational and social facilities for the city's black population, today Crispus Attucks serves the whole community with daycare, housing development, job training, and recreational services. The members of the congregation hoped for an opportunity to educate themselves and build relationships. During a tour of the building the director offered the congregation a home for worship for as long as it was needed, for free. Stunned, the congregational representatives wondered aloud how they could repay such generosity. The director shook his head, smiling, and replied quietly, "Isn't this the way it's supposed to be?"

In what ways can I receive humbly? ∼

O God, help me to remember that I do your work in both giving and receiving with humility.

JULY 19

Sometimes the call to generosity forces us outside our comfort zones. When the Hammerskin Nation—one of the new generation of white supremacist groups with websites and advance promotion of their events—announced a "benefit" concert, sixty people from all over the county converged near the proposed site to stage a Unity Rally in protest. To begin the rally, the convening minister said he would take an offering—something not usually done. But the stated purpose of the skinhead concert was to raise money for the widow and children of a member who had recently died of leukemia. Four hundred and fifty dollars was collected from the Unity demonstrators.

Is there a stone in my own heart that was really thrown by another? ∼

Dear God, help me meet hatred with compassion, injustice with persistence, and ignorance with a willingness to understand.

JULY 20

*Sometimes we judge others before knowing them.
People who might not ever know one another may
work on a common project, say, Habitat for Humanity,
and find a friend. Sharing in a common mission may
offer opportunities for discovering common ground. We
are more alike than different.*

Where can I search for someone who might be my ally
in the struggle for justice? ∽

May I remember in my frailty that I need not be alone.

JULY 21

The more we get to know someone different from us, the more likely we are to see similarities and to appreciate (rather than fear) differences. Rev. Kay Sorenson has a ministry to the homeless in San Francisco's Tenderloin District. In preparation for a "street retreat" Kay encourages youth to articulate what they think they'll find among the homeless. They generally list words like despairing, smelly, drugged-out, hopeless. *Then the young enter the park; their only mandate is to be there, to open themselves to the experience. After three hours they return to the church to process what they've done and seen. They list their impressions:* funny, courageous, smart, lost. *These young people have ventured through the doorway of transformation. Their presence with the "Other" in an attitude of listening has restored to them a deeper sense of their own humanity.*

Can I think of an experience I've had that truly transformed my perceptions and attitudes about another? ∼

Spirit of Unity, let my religion bind me to others in the understanding that we are responsible to one another.

JULY 22

In the Mexican border city of Juarez, a U.S. seminarian was beginning a six-month mission with the urban poor. The Mexican barrio worker doing orientation said to the student, "If you are here to save me, go home. If you are here to help me, go home. If you are here because you know your salvation is tied to my pain, then we can work together."

If a missionary came to my town to work in the "border-lands," where would I tell her to begin? ∼

Let me appreciate my freedom and the sacrifices of others and help me to remember that the struggle should not end until all people are free.

WHEN ALL SEEMS LOST, life at its bleakest, what pulls us through that desperate time? This is a question many of us have asked—particularly when life seems most difficult. Can we try to focus on what seems precious: flowers and fields, family and friends, light and life, darkness and rest? Sometimes we are able to pull through hard times alone, but more often it is others who help us through simply by walking with us. For many, there is a Guiding Presence or inner sense that gives courage and guidance. Each person may have that inner source of strength that shows the way from despair to hope and courage.

JULY 23

Sometimes the greatest lessons life teaches us are during times of what appear to us to be losses or failures. Learning this, we are renewed.

What helps pull us through difficult times? ∼

This candle that flickers, may it bring warmth and light. May the power of love from God and community be empowering. May my prayers join in a chorus with others.

JULY 24

Even in the midst of suffering, it is possible to refocus our energies, if only for a moment.

How can I shift my focus from fears to hopes? ∼

Help me to learn to look at life differently.

JULY 25

*At the Wellness Center, members of a support group
for cancer patients were sharing experiences, fears,
and joys. One member who had been fearful about
her treatment told us about her butterfly dream. She
was at the shore and saw a rock covered with migrat-
ing butterflies, huddled together against the ocean
wind. She wondered how they could travel so far with
such delicate wings. Then she thought, "If they can do
it, so can I."*

What models of courage have been my inspiration? ～

Let the courage and determination of others inspire me
and give me strength.

JULY 26

*In an English poem a child asks if dragons are real
and will come after him. The nurse hushes him, tells
him there are no dragons, and urges him to go to
sleep. The father, listening at the door, whispers that
dragons* are *real and prays that the boy, when older,
may face them with courage. Fear is a dragon, a roar-
ing spit-fire beast that makes our knees shake and
stomachs quake. Fear grows before our eyes, paralyz-
ing us. Elizabeth Barret Browning wrote: "The little
cares that fretted me, / I lost them yesterday. . . . / The
foolish fears of what may happen / I cast them all
away." She lost them in the fields of flowers, clover,
and grass. The beauty of the world took her fears
away.*

What things have helped soften my fears? ～

In the midst of fear may I think of a field of flowers high-
lighted by sun, and may their beauty shine through me.

JULY 27

Air Force fliers are taught repeatedly to grab at the correct side for their parachute release so that it becomes automatic. Doing things without thinking can be a lifesaver but it can also be destructive, such as when we always respond defensively or angrily. If we want the world to change and ourselves to change for the better, we must find new ways. It takes courage and determination to break pervasive patterns.

In what ways have I changed from destructive to constructive habits? ⌣

Give me the insight to see destructive habits and the courage to find a new way.

JULY 28

"There is a powerful and benign force at work within us, about us, at the interior of being and above it, which sustains our hope."

—GEORGE H. WILLIAMS

What brings me hope? ⌇

Focus and center me that I may discover the living stream of hope that runs deep within.

JULY 29

We often forget the daily graces of life, the providential givens—air to breathe, water to drink, work to be done, music to be heard, words to be spoken, choices to be made, food to be eaten, friends to be seen, books to be read, ideas to be thought, feelings to be shared, family to be loved, flowers to be noticed.

What are my daily graces of life? ⌇

Gratitude for life, for time, for energy, for family and friends, for that beloved community within yet beyond time, I give thanks.

"SYNCHRONICITY" IS A TERM coined by Carl Jung to refer to seemingly accidental life events that are tied together by the meanings we give them. These are acausal happenings, episodes that do not seem to follow the normal cause-and-effect processes. One can almost feel the flow of the interconnections and sometimes even laugh at them. A simple example will suffice. A father, trying to explain this concept to his son, concluded with the illustration that "if we start thinking about Ohio license plates, we will probably see one today." Within a minute, a car bearing an Ohio license plate drove by. Some oldtime Universalists might have given the label "Providence" to the synchronistic events that happen around us all the time.

JULY 30

Whether we call the principle of synchronicity Providence or God or the Tao or energy, it seems that there may be "laws" of the cosmos that we not only relate to but can change.

What examples of synchronicity have touched my life? ⌣

Sought or not sought, God is unfolding, if we have the heart to see and the wisdom to laugh. So let me watch my life, that I may grow in depth and understanding of that which is the Way.

JULY 31

*For a splendid example of synchronicity, we have only
to look to the history of Universalism. Think about
the awesome synchronicity of a fleeing English
preacher (John Murray) arriving on the shores of the
American coast "by accident," wandering into the
woods, and there encountering a Quaker-Baptist-
Universalist illiterate farmer (Thomas Potter) who
ten years previously had constructed a chapel for a
preacher of Universalism.*

What's a vision? ~

Vision of my heart, when all around me I find no outward
signs of success, keep in me a clear mind and heart, that
I may follow this dream as it unfolds before me.

AUGUST 1

Some believe American Unitarianism was born in Northumberland, Pennsylvania. There a chapel bearing the name of Dr. Joseph Priestley, scientist and minister, sat empty for many decades. Today, the chapel has been restored and a new congregation uses it because a few people worked to make the vision come alive.

Have I ever known beforehand that something major was going to happen in my life? ⌣

Help me to be ready to act on the future before it happens and to trust my intuition about what I must do to be whole.

AUGUST 2

*Almost thirty years ago, a man discovered a piece of
art thrown out by an art museum. He loved it so
much that he took it home and carried it with him
over the years, often wondering why he kept it. It happened to be a statue of Mary, the mother of Jesus, and
two boys. On yet another move, he decided to leave it
behind with a friend, who then decided to give it to a
ninety-one-year-old woman. He described her as
"stunned and speechless" when he presented her the
statue. Over fifty years ago, she had been the artist,
using herself and her two sons as models for the statue
of Mary, Jesus, and John. The chances of the statue
being returned were quite small, yet it was returned to
its owner and creator a half century later. It was a
homecoming, a meaningful connection, not necessarily one of cause and effect.*

Have I ever been surprised by what seemed to be a
strange twist of fate or chance happening? ∼

In a world that often seems victimized by chance, help
me to see from time to time the surprising touch of irony
and meaning.

AUGUST 3

"Don't think about pink elephants!" Of course, any-one hearing that injunction will immediately think about pink elephants, because the thought has been planted. In a similar way, synchronistic events seem to multiply the more we look for them, meaning either that they were there all the time but we were unaware of them or that our thinking about them somehow triggered other such happenings.

Can I remember today to look for synchronicities in my life—those small, seemingly insignificant events that catch me by surprise? ∽

Laughing Way, which tricks me by illusion and misdirection, teach me the path of watchfulness and attention to your flow in my life.

AUGUST 4

*If we are truly awake to life, then we will find in it
principles or laws or ways of being that seem more in
tune with the universe, so that we will not have to do
anything at all but stand there.*

When does my life seem "in the flow," easily lived,
simple? ⌒

Words cannot speak the truth. Symbols cannot capture
the truth. Religions can only point the way. O That
Which Is Forever, teach me humility and grace and
patience.

AUGUST 5

Every person, consciously or not, has experienced synchronicity, grace, providence—has experienced events that at the time seemed insignificant but that later were judged to be life-transforming. Every experience of synchronicity is an experience of grace, as if the universe is saying, "You are not alone." Grace happens.

What is providence? ⌣

I wish for myself the eyes to see, the ears to hear, and the heart to understand your presence in my life, O God, so that I might not be alone.

SOMETIMES WE TRY to make our way through life on intellect alone. We think the best way to avoid trouble is to anticipate things before we experience them. The words of Mark Twain sometimes ring true for us: "I have suffered many traumas in life, many of which I have never experienced." The flip side is that planning alone leads us nowhere. Learning takes place through experience. If we are lucky, we are given the opportunity to reflect upon the experience. And often what we reflect upon is not the experience at all, but our own perceptions of that experience. The human story can be expressed as action and reflection in a continuing cycle.

AUGUST 6

Do you remember the last time you tried something new and the experience opened a whole new world to you? Maybe you took a class in architecture, started attending church, began volunteering at the Humane Society, or acted in a local theater production. You may have found yourself thinking, "If only I had known what this experience would mean to me." New experiences can lead us into new worlds of insight and give us outlets for our personal passion for life. We can explore and choose ways to express our unique gifts.

Do I take time to appreciate the world as life unfolds before me, and do I take time to open new doors to ever-deepening experience? ∼

Lord of Revelation, encourage me to open new doors so as to gain insight into this miraculous life. Support me as I attempt new missions, exploring unknown territory in my heart, mind, and soul. Guide me in seeing each day as a glorious beginning.

Most people can think of moments in their lives that they regret. Learn to share your true compassion and love when you feel it. When you feel moved to tell others of your true feelings, strive to share them as honestly as possible. Tragedy will come in our lives; we cannot stop it. So don't wait—don't give yourself the chance to regret not sharing yourself.

Do I take the time to share with those I love my true feelings about them? ∼

Love's Heart, help me open myself to those I love and share my feelings. Help me to move beyond any fear or hesitation and embrace the world with warmth.

Some years ago a lake cottage was near abandonment. But with a new roof and a partial new floor, which brought the refrigerator up from the ground, the cottage was saved. Those who repaired the cottage found it needed an incredible amount of work: the scraping, caulking, priming, painting, and on and on. Now when people look at the white cottage with marine trim, they see its beauty. So much in life needs the constant attention of preservation and maintenance.

What situations in my life need constant attention? ∼

O God, help me to be aware of what needs my attention and the work that needs to be done.

AUGUST 9

As we grow older, our families and communities grow older as well. Children grow into adults and have their own children, and parents grow older and become grandparents and great-grandparents. The needs of family and community change as time passes for each member. You may find opportunities to learn from your elders and opportunities to mentor the young. Be patient with yourself and those around you as you all learn in growing and supporting one another.

Do I take the time to think about the changing needs of my elders and the children in my community, and do I think about how I can provide support and encouragement to them along their way? ⌣

Lord of our lives, show me how to be tender and encouraging, thoughtful and supportive in my family and my community. Being a reservoir of love creates broad support from which more love can grow.

AUGUST 10

"We must not only preach but live by what we had received as truth, or else renounce it honestly as impracticable."

—ADIN BALLOU

Is my life speaking what I hold to be true? ⌣

Spirit of Integrity, who knows me better than I know myself, keep me on the path of living my truth as deeply as I am able, making my life speak of that which I hold to be ultimate.

Western culture teaches that hard work receives the highest reward. Hard work entails long and consistent hours spent achieving goals and strategizing new successes. Our spiritual lives require a different type of hard work. The spiritual life cannot be scheduled. The effect of the Divine on our lives and on our spirits comes in small and large revelations, in love and support in times of sorrow and grief, in challenge in times of strength, inspiring us to be a light in the world. We cannot get to work at 7 A.M. and decide that we will achieve a certain spiritual level by noon. God may catch us up and reveal a new direction for our life, or maybe we will be given signs regarding a particular problem.

Do I make time to sit and be with Spirit, regardless of outcome or goals? ～

Lord, help me appreciate the blessed moments when I spend time talking to you and listening to you. Help me open my heart to unknown territory, to expose myself to you so that you can reveal to me all that I am meant to be here on earth.

It is important that we acknowledge our personal growth as we experience our journey through life. Some of us went to school and possibly college, maybe continuing this path by obtaining advanced degrees. Some went through a Catholic confirmation or a Bar Mitzvah. Some got married. We need to stop and celebrate these rites of passage, these precious times when we cross from one stage of life to another. As we grow older and change, our attitudes about life grow and change as well.

Have I taken the time to celebrate my growth and do I acknowledge my own inner changes? ∼

Great Spirit, help me look with new eyes at the important moments in my life, past and present. Help me acknowledge each achievement and each venture into a new phase of life, truly celebrating the miracle of personal development. Resonant within the fertile field of my soul, help me accept this personal joy of life with dignity and respect so that I can move on to new beginnings with revived energy and enthusiasm.

A JOKE OFTEN TOLD about Unitarian Universalists carries a message we might not want to hear: "Unitarian Universalists are quite tolerant people, really. They approach every subject with an open mouth." But what should we listen for? Some would say we should listen carefully to what we say to ourselves. Others would add that we must learn to listen to others. Some would say we need to listen to God. Listening is an art practiced over time. To listen to one's inner self, others, or God is as close as one's breath, and as difficult to see. Sometimes the best we can do is put ourselves in the presence of listening and sit still long enough to hear.

AUGUST 13

Practicing listening is the heart of the spiritual life. To hear is to comprehend. Taking time to listen is the beginning of wisdom.

When do I take time to listen to my heart's yearnings?

Help me to listen to myself, to others, and to God.

AUGUST 14

Find a place where you can sequester yourself from
disruptions (other people, telephones, etc.). In that
place, spend fifteen minutes listening to yourself.

What is my heart saying that, in the rush of things, I have
not been able to hear? ⌣

Slow me down so that I may learn to hear myself.

AUGUST 15

Find someone you want to hear and practice the art of listening by focusing on what he or she is saying to you. Do not think ahead of what you will respond to that person. Stay focused on what the person is saying.

How can I practice listening? ～

Spirit of Listening, help me to hear someone else before I speak, and to wait patiently without interrupting.

AUGUST 16

God is formed in us as we wait expectantly.

How does God speak to me? ∿

God beyond God, sound without a name, light without form, being beyond yet within, open my ears that I might hear and my heart that I might seek you.

AUGUST 17

Practicing listening is also praying without ceasing.

How can I remember today to practice the art of listening? ∿

God, help me to listen today so that I might hear myself, others, and you.

Alone together in solitude, listening with others, is a great spiritual resource. In the presence of shared listening, one learns to hear that which is not self.

Where can I go to practice listening? ∼

Help me to find others who will share with me the journey of listening, that I might be strengthened in mind, body, and spirit.

AUGUST 19

"God will be present, whether asked or not."

—LATIN PROVERB

When do I feel God's presence? ∼

When life is without beauty, and my sadness and despair deepen, I search for you but you cannot be found. Lead me to you. This wish is my prayer.

A teenaged girl decided right before entering college that she was not meant to go and never had been. She was sure that if she took four months off to perfect her study habits and separate more gradually from her boyfriend, she might be able to face it—for surely, she thought, no eighteen-year-old on the face of the planet was as messed up as she. Her parents said, "Ah, we know this place."

But when the crucial moment came, the young woman packed up and headed for college as planned. When she moved into her dorm, she called her mother and said, "I think I'm going to like it here. Her mother said, "Ah, I know this place."

In the morning she called her father, crying, saying she was too lonely to bear it. Her father said, "Ah, I know this place."

Change does not come in neat packages. It never has and it never will. Ah, we know this place.

What is stopping me from doing what I have always meant to do? ∽

Divine Spirit, help me to remember that life is full and rich and imperfect and that within all that is, I am whole as I move onward.

AUGUST 21

*Looking at the authenticity of how we express our-
selves in our daily world brings forth the issues
waiting for change. "What we resist persists," they say.
There is much fatigue caused by our resistance and by
the illusion that somehow we can control the flow of
events that create our life story.*

What am I resisting in my life? ⁓

In this moment of thoughtfulness and prayer, may I see
clearly what I am here to do.

TRANSITIONS FROM one condition, stage, form, activity, or place to another are everyday happenings woven inextricably into each person's life. The heart of transition is the actual moment in which this passage takes place. What makes transitions "blessed" is our ability to see them as sacred occurrences, discerning them with reverence as we acknowledge their happening. Sometimes fear drives us to try to avoid transitions. We see them as risks rather than opportunities. When we are successful in running away, we cut ourselves off from life's surprises, even the joyful ones, and thereby deprive ourselves of the new insights or paths that they open up to us.

AUGUST 20

When people declare that they are where they are by choice, the soil for change is made fertile.

How did I honor my last major transition? ∼

Sacred home, respect this place where I am in my life. Surround me with compassion and patience as I pay tribute to myself and those I love. Give me the courage to see past this fear as the unknown unfolds before me.

AUGUST 23

It has always been this way. It will never change.
People can't change. I can't change. I don't want to
change. I hate change. It won't make any difference.

What is one thing I can change for the better? ∼

Great Spirit, allow my skepticism and anger to leave
every cell in my body so that my eyes are made new
again. Help me to see.

AUGUST 24

There is a precious internal voice that speaks to us when it is the right time for transition to occur in our lives. It is a voice that, if ignored, causes us to make bad choices, denying us affirmation of the mystery of our being.

When have I ignored my internal voice? What happened? ～

May I be able to hear the voice of truth that speaks within me. May I bless it for the precious sounds it makes as it speaks to me. May I hold it in the highest regard as it lovingly points the way.

AUGUST 25

Every spring geese appear overhead, silently sweeping northward across the sky, as if in tune with some invisible mystery calling them home. They fly in a "V" pattern, honking messages of support to one another. They know more about timing, about when to act, than we do.

What is time? ∿

As I journey through life, help me to recognize when the time is right to act—and then help me act as I know I should.

AUGUST 26

Trust and faith and love and courage are great mates to have on life's journey.

Do I trust my decisions? ～

In this quiet moment may I have the courage and insight to know that life transitions are part of my journey, and that it can be enriched and blessed just by my saying so.

NONE OF US is exempt from suffering, though some carry a greater load than others. How we bear our suffering—how we understand it, work through it, and learn from it—determines its effect on us. None of us is allowed to choose our place of birth or the circumstances of our early lives. Some of us are born into situations that seem harsh; others are blessed with better situations. It is not just genetics and upbringing that set the story for our life adventure; it is how we work with what we have been given so that we, and often others, are transformed.

Buddhism addresses suffering head-on. The cause of suffering is the result of fighting against the bumpy road that is life. And the way through suffering comes neither to one who clings to the suffering (attachment) nor to one who pushes the suffering away with denial (detachment); rather, the way through suffering is to be nonattached. This attitude of nonattachment involves observing yet intentionally continuing along the path.

The wisdom of Buddhism lies in the companion piece to the theology of suffering. No one is expected to go alone. Three treasures accompany each sufferer: the Buddha, the Dharma, and the Sangha. The Buddha is the Holy One, the Dharma is the scripture, and the Sangha is the community of faith.

How do the three treasures appear in my life? Do I long for a beloved community to share with me a deep love of music, ancient teaching stories, and a coming together of these in worship, grounded in the Source, the Spirit of Life, and Love? ∼

O Great Spirit of Life and Love, give me courage to continue on the path you have set for me with acceptance and faith.

AUGUST 28

"Be of good cheer; it is I; be not afraid."

—MATTHEW 14:27

Who has come unexpectedly to be with me on my path?
If suffering, grief, and loss have separated me from
friends or family members, are there new people coming
into my life? Can I see in their faces the presence of the
Divine Source? ∽

O Holy One, who comes in the guise of ordinary people,
teach me to be conscious in this time which so often
feels chaotic and out of control. Show me your face, that
your presence may give me courage.

AUGUST 29

*A common theme in the experience of mystics—
Eastern and Western, ancient and modern—is the
discovery of the sacred in the midst of the ordinary.*

Do I know someone who has suffered for a long time
and come to trust God's compassionate love and lasting
forgiveness for human error? Often ordinary kindnesses,
thoughtfully included in the routine of the day, open a
sacred door. Are these healing moments? ⌣

O Sacred Presence, enter into the rooms of suffering.
Grant me the wisdom to make my ordinary tasks acts of
compassionate love. Make me the hands and feet of
Grace.

The arrival of the unexpected is the mystery and challenge of being on the path.

Do I shrink from the presence of the unexpected? In times of suffering, grief, and loss, has the unexpected too often brought tragedy? As the journey of my healing moves, as unexpected companions join me (perhaps briefly to share a gift and depart), do I seek in each day an unexpected gift, a soft breeze, a quiet act of kindness, a sunset? *Sit quietly, for five minutes holding an image of quiet beauty from today.*

Spirit of Life and Love, move in my life in a gentle way. Teach me to see in simple things the gift in the unexpected.

AUGUST 31

"Ye thought evil against me; but God meant it unto good."

When families endure suffering, grief, and loss, pleas for forgiveness may be premature, even unthinkable. Can reconciliation be sought before forgiveness? Not clinging, not denying, is reconciliation the first step, doable in the moment? ⌣

God of Mercy and Love, help me know a lasting forgiveness in your Sacred Presence. Help me leave aside demands for a perfect and total forgiveness beyond my human capacities. Grant me knowledge of your unconditional love, that I may accept myself and others.

SEPTEMBER 1

*In the midst of suffering, valued relationships may be
strained as we seek to assign blame for every wrong
or hurt suffered. And yet because suffering is integral
to life, blame is never the central issue.*

Can I forgive myself for what I did not know, for what
I chose not to know? Can I then offer that limited
forgiveness to others? ∼

In the midst of suffering, teach me, O Holy One, to
understand that not everything may be blamed on
someone—whether myself or others. Teach me to return
to the wisdom that Life is an uneven road.

SEPTEMBER 2

"The angel which redeemed me from all evil, bless the lads."

—GENESIS 48:16

Can we find a creative way to reveal family secrets to our children without passing on to them the curse of blame? Can we offer our children balance—not hiding our sorrow but still offering them hope? Would the character of suffering be changed if family secrets and their companion, shame, could be replaced in children by reconciliation and peace? ∼

El Shaddai, God of Joseph, how very good and pleasant it is when kindred live together in unity. Help the members of my family and community to accept each other. Teach us to raise up our children in a way that invites reconciliation and peace.

BEING MINDFUL of each day—understanding that each day is a gift—is the attitude that brings receptivity to prayer and the rhythms of living. Emptiness, solitude, loneliness, absence, despair—these are our teachers, too. It has been written that the teacher appears when the student is ready. We always feel ready for the advent of joy, but few of us are ready for the teachers of negativity, who show us the way through the days we are given as being fraught with struggle. It's hard to acknowledge that we know ourselves more deeply when we walk a hard and difficult path and rejoice at the end in having made it through.

SEPTEMBER 3

"Neither a single atom nor a single soul can get beyond the reach of this Almighty force of love so that it is unable to draw back."

—QUILLEN HAMILTON SHINN

Is there anything that really lasts forever? ∿

Power of Love in the universe, though I cannot know anything for certain, I feel your presence in my life and in the lives of those dearest to me. Help me to see a presence greater than death so that I may live without fear.

SEPTEMBER 4

*It is very difficult—seemingly impossible sometimes—
to forgive those who have wounded us deeply and to
forget the transgressions. No matter how deep the
hurt, however, one enduring principle of living seems
to be that we cannot go on until we do forgive, if not
forget.*

Who has wounded me deeply through the years? Are
there any among them whom I have not yet forgiven? ∿

*Write down the names of the persons who have wounded
you deeply. Then tear the list up after saying the following
prayer*: Let these people and the wounds they caused no
longer have power over my life. I release them and
myself into your care.

SEPTEMBER 5

*What may often appear to be endings in life are really
new beginnings, which we seldom understand until
later. The old must be transformed to make the new.*

In my own life, when have endings actually been
beginnings? ∼

Teach me to die so that I might live. Help me to let go
so that I might find new life. And through all the transitions, steady and secure me in your love.

SEPTEMBER 6

When things fall apart, we generally try to hold them together. However, we may make matters worse in trying to make them better. Sometimes things must *fall apart before they can be put back together. At such times, in letting go we rediscover ourselves and our reasons for being.*

When have I let go of a problem, and what happened? ∽

Let go, let go, let go—and see what happens.

SEPTEMBER 7

Let fall come. It is time to prepare for the great waiting, the inner cleansing, the falling away of old dreams, and the preparation of new ones. Let winter chill my unrealistic expectations with blessed solitude. Deep down in the whiteness, bring me back to myself. Let there be spring in my heart; let images of new sprouts, the flight of returning birds, and the plowing of new fields give me strength to begin again. Let the warm winds of summer settle in my spirit. Slow down, slow down: take time to be whole.

What season of my life am I in now? ⌒

Lord of the Dance, let seasons come and go in my life, but within let me know that something remains.

SEPTEMBER 8

"Lo, I am with you alway, even unto the end of the world."

Have I ever experienced a moment in life that seemed timeless? ⌣

O Divine Being, present in all times and in all ages and among all people, known by different names and recounted in different languages, and worshipped in diverse ways, be in my time, too, that I might understand myself in the light of your purpose. Be with me now and implant in my spirit a lasting conviction that I am not alone.

SEPTEMBER 9

We need to seek forgiveness for our weaknesses and failures—for judging others more harshly than we judge ourselves, for pointing out the shortcomings of others while forgetting our own, for being slow to act for justice but quick to meet our own needs, for sowing conflict by not speaking up, and for professing spiritual values while not heeding the spirit.

What are my shortcomings? ⁓

Create in me a clear and contrite heart, and let me judge myself before judging others and look to my motivations before criticizing others.

IN THE STILLNESS of your sacred space, no matter where that might be, take time to be quiet, centered, at one with yourself and others. It is important for each of us to have a space of our own, where we can spend time alone, without interruptions. This need not be a physical space; it can be a place inside us that we can retreat to even when surrounded by activity. In such spaces, we feel at home with ourselves, focused, and connected to that which is holy. It is possible and necessary for you to find such space in order to be whole.

SEPTEMBER 10

A sacred space can be a place, with another person, walking outside, listening to or playing music, or just sitting quietly by yourself.

Where is my sacred space? ⌒

In silence, go within until you find a still, quiet place. Stay there for a few moments before leaving, and mark its location in your soul.

Whatever else religion might be, if it does not have at its source a living connection to that which is holy and ultimate, it is not whole.

Do I feel a living connection to that which is holy? ∽

Source of Life, power that moves in and between people, keep this feeling alive in me and in others, so that I may be whole. Disrupt my deadly routines. Blast my arrogance away.

SEPTEMBER 12

Propositions: (1) We did not make ourselves, nor were we accidents. We were formed in the image of the Creative Power that initiated everything. (2) We have turned away from that Creative Power. (3) We sometimes feel our connections to that power, but we need others to help us. (4) The purpose of a spiritual community is to help us feel our connections to the Creative Power and to each other.

What are a few of the major propositions that I have found to be true? ⌒

Source of light and energy, let that original fire burn in me, and help me to understand that there is more illumination when my light is shared with others.

SEPTEMBER 13

"And on the seventh day, God ended his work...and he rested....And God blessed the seventh day, and sanctified it."

—GENESIS 2:2–3

Where can I find rest? ∼

Now is the appointed time to restore my soul.

SEPTEMBER 14

Everyone needs a place to retreat from worry. At a lake retreat, one is filled up with scanning the sky for storms, pruning willows, finding out about purple loose strife control, meditating in the hammock, fishing for sunnies, watching midnight lightning, brushing sand from our sheets, and taking time to breathe in this beauty. There is no room for fear or worry. They do not live at the lake. Let us look for ways to carry this sanctuary of peace everywhere.

Where do I find inward peace? ∿

Let the peace found within my heart serve as a wellspring for living.

SEPTEMBER 15

The sanctuary many people find in nature can also be found within. An old spiritual workbook had these words: "I have a blessed home in myself where I can go in and shut the door and kneel to my Father in secret and be at peace as a great Sea of Calm while all around and about is seeing trouble." Even in the midst of urban chaos, we can find the peace of the Sea of Calm in our deepest selves.

How can I find a quiet cove each day where I can be at peace? ∼

May I find the commitment and strength each day to create a place within where I can be at peace with Spirit and protected from the storms around me.

SEPTEMBER 16

"Take heed that ye do not your alms before men, to be seen of them."

—MATTHEW 6:1

Is there a place at home or work where I can go off by myself to pray? *If so, go there. If not, make a place in your mind and heart.* ⌒

In the stillness of the inner sanctuary, where I am alone with myself, let me feel the presence of the Divine as a parent comforting a child, and let me stay in the light when I take leave, still alone but no longer lonely.

A SEVENTY-TWO-YEAR-OLD MAN is dying. He sits in his living room talking to the hospice chaplain. This is their third visit. He looks up and notices that it has stopped raining. He invites the chaplain to take a walk around the block with him. Although he moves slowly outdoors, there is buoyancy in his step. He no longer fights the persistent force of sleep. He chats, asks the chaplain questions about her theological training, and inquires about what questions most occupy her study and spiritual life. He directs the conversation, keeping his feelings at bay. At the completion of his walk, he claims that he needs to rest. As he turns to enter the door of his home, he extends his hand. He smiles faintly, says good-bye, and adds, "I guess we're getting acquainted so that later we can discuss more substantial things."

SEPTEMBER 17

"Words are, of course, the most powerful drug used by mankind."

—RUDYARD KIPLING

When have I experienced my words as healing or hurtful? ∽

May my words become sources of healing for others.

SEPTEMBER 18

"Though conversing face to face, their hearts have a thousand miles between them."

—CHINESE PROVERB

How can I learn to connect more fully with others? ∼

Healing Presence, I know that there are times when I avoid those whose suffering I fear. Teach me compassion, so that I may speak the words that will bring me closer to them.

SEPTEMBER 19

"A wise man hears one word and understands two."
—JEWISH PROVERB

When was the last time I had a "substantial" conversation, one in which there existed a blend of heart and mind? ∽

Let me be both wise and honest in my listening. Let me hear not only the spoken word, but give me the power to comprehend the messages of the heart.

SEPTEMBER 20

*"The way from God to a human heart is through a
human heart."*

—SAMUEL GORDON

When have I opened my heart to the power of human
connection? ∼

I thank you, praise you, and rejoice in your abundance.
Bless me with a generous Spirit so that I may see in others not the stranger but the friend.

Where can wisdom be discovered and understanding found?

What sources of wisdom guide my life? ～

Tell me, how should I live? Show me another way.

SEPTEMBER 22

*We are interconnected to one another, whether we
consciously know so. Life may be short and sometimes
very difficult, but if we understand our connections to
one another, we should draw solace and strength from
the bonds of affection that may result. Kindness makes
and keeps us human in the deepest and best part of
our selves.*

When was the last time someone showed kindness to
me? ∼

May compassion be shown to me and kindness be the
gift I offer others, now and through all the days of my
life.

SEPTEMBER 23

"I said to the stones distinctly, not in a whisper: 'Give me your strength, so that I may feel again; for griefs have consumed me and made me lean.'"

—EXEKIEL HAKOHEN

When have I sought the strength of others? ∽

There are times when I barely know what I need and so am without words to ask for help. Give me the words to express my pain and the strength to speak them. I know that I cannot live without you.

IN A WORLD that favors overnight delivery and seeks instant gratification, patience is a rare and little-valued commodity, and yet patience remains one of the most valuable virtues. Bringing a dream to fruition, shaping a work-product with care, pursuing spiritual growth—all of these goals (and much more that we value in the world) take time to be realized. Real change takes both time and revolutionary patience. We must realize that many small steps will be required before the victory is won, whether it be for better housing, schools, jobs, or any other form of social justice. The great dreams are sown by visionaries but often not realized in their own lifetimes.

SEPTEMBER 24

"And he said, So is the kingdom of God, as if a man should cast seed into the ground; And should sleep, and rise night and day, and the seed should spring and grow up, he knoweth not how."

—MARK 4:26–27

How patient am I? ∼

Help me to learn to wait and rest and watch for that which takes time to mature, that I may grow from the inside out.

SEPTEMBER 25

Most of us do violence to ourselves by keeping more busy than we should, trying to do everything well, not taking time seriously enough to slow down and wait.

When do I slow down? ～

Listen, my soul, to your cries for solace and rest and patience.

A great deal of personal and spiritual growth takes place out of sight, underneath the surface, deep in the soil in which souls mature. It is a "law" of our spiritual lives that each one of us needs to care for our souls, because no one else will do that for us, and each of us needs to learn the art of being patient with ourselves and not doing more violence to our spirits by always keeping busy. The temptation is to do great things and accomplish much and win applause in the eyes of others. But life teaches us that what we consider great may not be so important, that our accomplishments recede in importance when we are alone, and that what others think of us is not as important as what we think of ourselves.

How do I take care of my soul? ∿

Help me, Spirit of Living, to take care of my soul and be someone, not violating my spirit by unrealistic expectations of myself and others, but showing kindness and temperance and patience toward myself and all those with whom I share life.

*Thomas Potter, the farmer who built a chapel in 1760
for the Universalist preacher John Murray, who didn't
arrive until ten years later to give his sermon in
Potter's meetinghouse, would have understood better
than most of us the images of planting and sowing
and waiting patiently. His hopes were high—he
"believed the future in"—but he knew enough to
know that his timing was not God's and that in good
time his prayers would be answered.*

What has it been like for me to plant a dream or idea
and wait? ~

God of waiting times, grant me patience to wait without
idols, not forcing reality to bend to my needs, but staying
in tune with the flow of time and living the faith
between the dream and the reality.

SEPTEMBER 28

*Sometimes the best we can do is to remain awake
and watchful, aware that what passes for success in
the eyes of the world is not necessarily what feeds the
soul. To wait and watch is difficult. Most people
either drown out the inner sense with increased activity or deaden all senses. To wait and watch is to know
that life at its deepest requires of us steady hearts,
clear minds, and patient spirits.*

How do I keep watch over my soul? ∼

God of my restless soul, be still in me, that I may find
food for my spirit in quiet and patient watchfulness.

SEPTEMBER 29

In 1861, Olympia Brown arrived at St. Lawrence Theological School to study for the ministry, surprising the seminary president, who thought that he had discouraged her from enrolling. After becoming the first woman to be denominationally ordained, Olympia Brown became an advocate for the right of women to vote. It was not until 1920, at the age of eighty-five, that Olympia Brown was able to cast her first ballot.

What dream of mine has been deferred? ∼

Teach me to keep the dream alive within, even when there are no outward signs of its potential, and let me have revolutionary patience, knowing that when I am not divided within all is well.

SEPTEMBER 30

Wait and watch. Watch and wait. And when the time is ripe, act.

How can I know when is the right time to act? ∼

Watchful and Waiting Spirit, so direct my inward sense that I may learn to keep still until it is time to act.

AFTER CREATING THE WORLD, even God is reported to have spent a day resting (see Genesis 2:2). Jesus also felt the need to rest and take time for prayer: "And in the morning, rising up a great while before day, he went out, and departed into a solitary place, and there prayed" (Mark 1:35). The purpose of taking time for solitude and prayer is to commune with that which is not the self, which some call the voice of God. We need to take time to be solitary, especially in an age such as ours, with its demands on our time, its bombardments of noise, and its constant desire that we remain busy, often to the exclusion of our deepest spiritual needs.

Ironically, our Sundays often do not feed our souls. We rush off to worship, we spend a hectic social time, and then we rush home to the television set.

Sabbath means "rest." The familiar words of the Twenty-Third Psalm strike a receptive chord in most of us, expressing a yearning to care for our spirits. "He maketh me to lie down in green pastures; he leadeth me beside still waters. He restoreth my soul. . . . " As a way to achieve that spiritual rest, practice the presence of God in your life this week by making space, solitude.

Future weeks are structured with opening words, a question to prompt reflection, and a closing meditation or prayer. But in this first week, each day will begin with a suggested exercise so that you may make a "little sabbath." You may find different ways to enter the inner sanctuary. It is not the ritual that matters, but its purpose: communion with God.

OCTOBER 1

Find a place in your heart or a physical space where you can be alone. Settle in for five minutes and listen. Close with words of prayer or meditation.

OCTOBER 2

Rather than watching a half-hour of television or reading, take that time to stay in silence. When words or sounds interrupt your prayerfulness, let them pass over lightly.

OCTOBER 3

Tie a string around your finger or find some other way to jar your memory, so that sometime in the day, wherever you are, you find five minutes to stay in silent prayer.

OCTOBER 4

Read the following and meditate on it for five minutes.

"The Lord is my Shepherd; I shall not want.
   He maketh me to lie down in green pastures:
   He leadeth me beside the still waters.
   He restoreth my soul:
   He leadeth me in the paths of righteousness for His
   name's sake.

   Yea, though I walk through the valley of the shadow
   of death,
   I will fear no evil: For thou art with me;
   Thy rod and thy staff they comfort me.
   Thou preparest a table before me in the presence of
   mine enemies;
   Thou anointest my head with oil; My cup runneth
   over.

Surely goodness and mercy shall follow me all the days
   of my life.
   and I will dwell in the House of the Lord forever."

PSALMS 23:1–6

OCTOBER 5

Take one issue or life problem that is troubling you now, focus on it, and ask for guidance. Do so in silence.

OCTOBER 6

Whether you are eating alone or with others at dinner, ask that the meal begin with three minutes of silence, after which time anyone may mention something or someone for which he or she is thankful. If you wish, light a candle at the end and say amen.

OCTOBER 7

Spend time in solitude and prayer, and when you feel that the time is ended, jot down a few words or sentences that describe what this week has been like for you.

THE DEVOTIONAL LIFE begins with you, but it does not end there. Only you know where you are on life's way, and though solitude and silence are paths along the way, they lead into relationships with others and with what you consider to be Holy. Continuing the solitary journey is essential, but if continued in isolation, it can be insulating and hazardous to your deepening process.

OCTOBER 8

There is a natural inclination to want to be with others who can reflect on and assist your growth. As you explore the many paths that you encounter in life, share the struggles, the adventures, and the learning with those you encounter along the way.

Why is the devotional life more than the personal? ⌒

In deepening my own life of devotion, keep me from that kind of selfish pride that makes me feel better than others, and let me find others who can help me walk the journey.

OCTOBER 9

Talk with someone who will listen to the language of your soul (Who am I? What am I spending my life for? In what do I place my trust? How do I find strength for daily living?) is what some would call "spiritual friendship." If there is no one in your life who is already filling this need, there is someone who could if he or she were asked. This role need not be in traditional terms a "spiritual director," but simply someone you can go to from time to time, knowing that he or she will both hear what you are saying and respond with honesty and support.

To whom might I express my deepest spiritual needs? ∼

In truth and light, help me to find kindred spirits who know me from the inside out and can lend me eyes and heart as I travel life's journey.

OCTOBER 10

Some of the earliest forms of being together with others in spiritual community were what were then called "conventicles," or small groups meeting together weekly to read the Bible, pray, and talk. George de Benneville's house church in Pennsylvania was one such conventicle, bringing together people from various religious sects for worship. De Benneville, and others after him, believed that this kind of gathering represents the form closest to the early Christian house church. Today, these kinds of house churches continue across and outside mainstream denominations, bringing together, in very small groups, literally millions of people.

Can I envision being part of a house church? ⌒

Where one or two are gathered together, there (we are told) is more. Help me to find this depth in my life.

Finding a spiritual community in which you can be accepted for who you are while also being challenged to grow is one of the most important experiences in life. Unfortunately, the search can be frustrating. Some communities seem to take an "anything goes" stance, leaving participants confused and without support. Others favor a straight and narrow path but lack heart and expansiveness. You will know when you are "home" spiritually when you no longer feel divided within yourself.

Where, if anywhere, do I feel divided no more? ∼

Help me to find that community where my heart and mind are one and where I am restored and renewed for life.

The old-time Universalists knew that faith was a matter of right living ("orthopraxis") and not just right believing ("orthodoxy"), though both concepts are interrelated. The spiritual life, then, is a way of living as much as a way of believing, a path of being as much as a path of thinking.

What are the values or principles that guide my life? 〜

Implant deep in my being the understanding that how I live is just as important as what I say I believe and that how I treat others is as expressive of my values as how I treat myself.

OCTOBER 13

Listening to another person's spiritual journey is a path that helps not only the other person but also yourself. In hearing another's journey, you are aware not only of connections to that person but also of the uniqueness of that life.

Can I find one person today and spend time listening to his/her journey? ∼

Help me to listen.

OCTOBER 14

A "little sabbath" is a time to restore the self. To feel restored in the presence of others is a blessing. A spirit-filled congregation is a community of blessings.

When was the last time I felt my spiritual community to be a blessing? ⁓

Spirit of Community, keep us mindful of why we come to find meaning and friendships in your midst and thankful for the opportunity of gathering with others.

THE "THREADS OF RELATIONSHIPS" form the tapestry of each person's life, connected over time by the weaving of our own hands. Our lives are about the connections we make within ourselves and within others. Sometimes we are not even aware that we have made these connections, but they are vital to the shape and colors of our lives. Every piece of the woven tapestry is connected, whether we can see the connections or not, whether we consider the weaving important or not. The interconnected web of life, of which we are a part, is both complex and full of wonder.

OCTOBER 15

City yards often extend right back to the alley. No fence prevents entry—just the loose cluster of elements such as shed, compost bin, lilac bush, and picnic table. Neighbors walking their dogs stroll by; children cut through on their boisterous walk home from school. This place is the loom on which we weave our neighborhood.

Where do I weave relationships with those around me? 〜

Let me hold in my heart as sacred the places of human connection.

OCTOBER 16

The director of the shelter for battered women called a minister to ask her to do a memorial service for one of their clients who'd died from a drug overdose. The dead woman's support group was afraid that because she was from another state no one would remember her. After the service the minister took a flower home, placed it on her kitchen windowsill, and spoke the dead woman's name when she saw the flower each morning. The flower bloomed for 26 days. How quickly and easily we can become nameless—even to ourselves.

Do I take the time occasionally to remember me to myself, speaking my name out loud? ∼

O God, when I feel alone, let me be comforted in the knowledge that you have called me by my name.

OCTOBER 17

Once there was a little girl whose mother sent her to the corner store for milk. Her instructions were clear: Go straight to the store, and hurry back. When the little girl returned with the milk but far past her mother's expected time, she was scolded by an angry, worried parent. "Why did you take so long?" Her daughter answered, "I saw Ashley. Her doll was broken, so I stopped to help."

"I told you not to stop. You couldn't fix her doll anyway," her exasperated Mother declared. "I know," the little girl replied, "I helped her cry."

When was the last time I listened to my own tears? ∼

May my capacity for compassion be not only for others.

We wake up to a new morning more than twenty thousand times in a lifetime, if we're lucky. And some of us are greeted with birdsong each of those many mornings.

What is dependable in my life? ∽

I affirm the interdependent web of existence of which I am a part.

OCTOBER 19

Even the most discordant color finds its place in a
tapestry.

Is there a shocking pink or dishwater brown I wish
I didn't have to work with? ∿

Spirit of Life, grant that the threads of relationship I
weave be not a tangle but a tapestry.

OCTOBER 20

One bumper sticker conveys a succinct statement of ministry: "The most radical thing we can do is introduce people to one another."

If Jesus was radical and Gandhi, with his nonviolence, was radical, what is my own radical action in the weaving of community? ∿

As I stretch my wings in flight, may I remember that it takes strength to fly with the flock and courage to stick one's neck out.

OCTOBER 21

Many grandmothers have taught youngsters how to deconstruct woolen garments, tear them into strips, and braid them into beautiful, serviceable rugs. What started as economic necessity has become for the children and grandchildren of these old women a spiritual practice, a source of comfort and renewal.

As I gather the worn scraps of a troubling relationship or situation in my life, how can I reweave them into something new? ∼

Help me to keep in mind that, as the craftsman braids torn finery, so a second chance can re-knit shredded dignity.

THE MAXIM "Keep it simple; it will get complex all by itself" applies to our prayer lives as well as our worldly lives. While it may be easy to see the wisdom of the words, it's difficult indeed to put them into practice. One person thinks there's not enough time in the day to practice five devotional minutes. Another believes day follows day without need of prayer. But the fact is that each one of us requires devotional time, and without it, we do not feel whole. To take time for one's soul is to take time to be fully human, attentive to life and its movement.

OCTOBER 22

"In the morning, rising up a great while before day, he went out, and departed into a solitary place, and there prayed."

—MARK 1:35

Where can I be alone but not lonely? 〜

Settle me down while I am able to keep watch over my being. Let me not be drawn to busy work and hectic schedules, but for only a moment or two each day take time to keep communion with myself and with God, lest I be swallowed by time and space.

OCTOBER 23

"Rest in the Lord, and wait patiently for him."

—PSALM 37:7

Where can I find rest that restores my very soul? ∽

Rest and restore me, God, that I may be renewed to do your work of love in the world.

OCTOBER 24

"He maketh me to lie down in green pastures: he leadeth me beside the still waters. He restoreth my soul."

—PSALM 23:2–3

What restores my soul? ∽

Lead me to find within myself the clarity of mind and renewal of spirit that I need to be whole in this world, which makes so many demands on me. Restore my soul.

OCTOBER 25

*There are times when there seem to be no answers
that satisfy, when the good stumble and the destructive prosper, when those who seem to dislike us
suddenly have power over us to do harm. At those
times, we can only pray for the strength to go on.*

When have I felt most abandoned and alone and under
attack? ⌣

Give me strength to make it through the day and to rest
at night.

OCTOBER 26

When we feel most alone and vulnerable, we can draw strength from the Holy Presence; it is always there, always accessible, if we are receptive.

Where do I find strength to live my values in the world? ∽

Presence, which is there even when I am unaware, grant me strength to live with dignity and integrity in the midst of a world that honors neither. *In silence, be aware of the Presence in you now.*

OCTOBER 27

The following prayer mirrors the feelings many of us have had in troubled times: "God, I have lost sight of you. I do not feel your presence as I once did. If I had never felt your presence, this absence would not be so disturbing. But you have visited me. You have lifted me out of bondage into the light of a new day. Now I pray that I may wait without idols and be satisfied with such light that I have already seen."

Can I "know" God from God's absence? ∽

In the wasteland of the heart, where I feel no presence, help me to remember and be thankful for those moments when I have felt your love.

OCTOBER 28

Give God time.

Just for today, how much time can I give to God? ∽

Eternal God, time is a precious gift for which I give thanks. Though my hurried life is lived often by the clock, let me give you one more minute each new day until my time becomes yours.

MEMORIES ARE the heart's anchor, a way of discovering our roots in a world that seems at times to lack stability as people come and go in our lives and we move from place to place. Memories are the heart's anchor for spiritual communities, too, a way of telling newcomers: Here is where we have been, and these are our stories. Without personal or communal memories, individuals and communities often feel incomplete and sometimes even hollow.

Because many people forget the people, places, and events of their early years, some parents keep a memory box for each child, full of report cards and drawings and pictures and similar treasures. That memory box becomes the child's link with the past.

If someone were keeping a memory box for me, what would I hope they would put inside? ⌣

God of my deepest memories, let me not forget that I am called by name and known.

OCTOBER 30

*The earliest memories of church or synagogue or tem-
ple are often not the ones we might suppose we would
remain—memories of what was taught formally (the
dogma, the history). Rather, our earliest memories
generally center on the feeling of the community, the
lighting of candles, the moments of silence, the way
people treat each other, the times when we laughed,
the times when people died.*

What are my earliest memories of my religious community (or, if I was not raised in any tradition, what adult
memories do I have regarding worship)? ∼

Teach me to live by light and life and thereby implant in
our children memories of hope and delight.

OCTOBER 31

*Family rituals form important memories—especially
rituals that set apart time for prayer or meditation or
sharing. Some families, for example, light a candle
each evening before sharing a meal, holding hands
and giving thanks. That ritual gives participants
pause to remember the blessings of life and to hear
each other.*

What family rituals do I remember having as I grew
up? ∼

Grateful for life, I remember especially those who share
in my journey from day to day. Let me not neglect or
harm them but remain steadfast in love.

NOVEMBER 1

Memories are the clues to our identity and to the contours of our present behaviors; they are also the materials out of which our futures are shaped.

What memories do I hope will remain for me well into the future? ∽

Make of my days good memories, that I may not be afraid of living or of dying.

NOVEMBER 2

Stories are the spiritual anchors for our memories.

What are the stories of my spiritual journey—its characters and plot and major crises? ∿

Keeper of Stories, remember me.

NOVEMBER 3

In dreams and daydreams, times when the imagination takes over, we are transported to what seems an invisible world—a world that always surrounds us but of which we are not aware. In this world of poets and visionaries and dreamers, we often discover memories of past times and events, and of different layers of Being than we know in the visible and tangible world. For lack of a better word, we seem part of a Great Memory of which we are an interconnected part, one link in a Great Chain of Being.

What was my last dream? ⌣

Help me to feel my connections to other times and places and people—connections that are deeper than waking and wider than one lifetime. Help bring to life in me, if only for this moment, the "communion of saints" or "beloved community," within which there is neither time nor space.

NOVEMBER 4

"For where your treasure is, there will your heart be also."

—MATTHEW 6:21

Where is my "treasure"? ∼

Teach me to forsake all lesser gods for the sake of my heart's treasure and to keep this wisdom deep in my memory, where neither time nor space can take it again.

EACH OF US has the right to at least one special place where we feel safe and secure, a place that offers us comfort even when we are far away. That place—whether it is a bricks-and-mortar house, an outdoor haven, or a state of mind, is home. Home is where we can go when we feel the need to be restored, whether it be a loved one's house, an apple orchard, or a church sanctuary. And over time, our places of refuge may change, but the feeling that we are blessed within that place is unchanging and reliable. When we are home, we know it.

NOVEMBER 5

For one young girl, home was an apple orchard with branches directed low for harvest and climbing. She and her friends climbed all summer, making private homes in the branches. They stayed on the ground as fall approached, building forts in the morning and having apple fights in the afternoon. In winter the skeleton trees were ignored; school became a new home. But steadfast, the apple trees were there again come summer, growing only as fast as the children's own legs, that they might continue to climb.

Somehow, for better and for worse, a first home establishes what we understand as normal or "homelike." What were some good things about the place where I grew up? ⌣

We are blessed with friends and geography, with life and memory. Hold in my heart the best memories. Let them live in me when I see children play. Let them be etched on my eyelids when I am tired and discouraged, as a reminder that I am a child of God.

NOVEMBER 6

Few of us are good at moving. Feeling "at home"
comes slowly, building over years, not weeks or
months, whether we are affiliating with a new
church, tackling new work, or settling into a new
neighborhood. Frustration and loneliness precede
at-homeness nearly every time. Then one day, as if the
air has suddenly cleared, it feels right to be in the new
place. Perhaps our willingness to uproot despite the
challenges is an example of faith that change will be
okay, that patience will prevail, and that a return to
home will come.

How long has it taken me to feel at home in my newest
place? Where was the holy in the transition? ⁓

My world changes around me; my pictures no longer fit
on my walls. Be with me, God, inspiring patience in my
heart to know that I will again feel at home, even in a
different place.

NOVEMBER 7

Moses and the Hebrew people wandered for forty years without a permanent home, watching for a sign that their home was near. The Hebrew people worried about the basics such as food, water, and rules for community, while sustaining a determination that they could reach their Promised Land. Sometimes we yearn for a pillar of light to guide us—a concrete, visible, tangible sign—but are unwilling to live in a tent and launch a journey toward our own Promised Land. And yet perhaps we forego big signs if we stay sheltered and safe.

What would it take to have the determination of the Hebrew people? ⟡

Keep me safe, Holy Protector, but not so safe as to miss every sense of call. Keep me sheltered, but not so sheltered that I miss the journey. Help me to know that a temporary home is enough, that each day on the journey is enough.

NOVEMBER 8

*In our lives there are many times we leave home. We
leave home and go to school—perhaps to kinder-
garten, perhaps to college. We leave again and create
our own home. We leave classmates and friends and
move across the country to start a new life. Tears flow
at leave-takings, even when we celebrate where we
are going next, because we must let go of people
whom we have loved in a way not likely to be recovered. Some say such departures are preparation for
dying. Perhaps so, but they are also preparation for
living with trust that we will be okay on the journey.*

At what turns on the road have I felt that I was leaving
home? What kept me rooted? ⌣

Holding life lightly, help me to release the past—the
good and the less pretty—that I may truly leave. Let me
pack in my boxes the things that will build me up as I
move on. Let me not pack the resentments and upsets.
Let me leave with trust that my next steps will be good
and sure and right.

NOVEMBER 9

We stomp on the floor to quiet the neighbor below; we keep a broomstick handy for banging on the ceiling above. Home is not always serene, not always a refuge. Doors slam; people shout; music blares. People face conflict—even within our space, our floor, our home. We often idealize the notion of "home," feeling that we are falling short if home is less than peaceful, less than perfectly considerate, less than a constant refuge. Sometimes those intrusions on the image of home are beyond our control. Sometimes they simply reflect the intensity of living in relationship. Creating comfort in chaos, the perfect in imperfection, may be our calling.

What do I need to thrive in my home space? ⌣

O Sustainer of Life, you call me to exercise patience and faith—perhaps courage, too, to know and to speak my needs, and perhaps generosity, to make space for the needs of those I love. Help me to love my neighbor, my family, my home life. Help me to find the good in all I interact with this day.

We walk in and know that we are home. It might be the fifty-third house with the real estate agent; it might be the sanctuary of a church. But we know, deep in the well of our knowing, that we were meant to stay. Something inside us relaxes. Something inside us celebrates this homecoming. The spaces, the light, the order finally make sense.

Do I feel that I have found home? ⌣

May the air of this space fill me with peace. May the light of this space cast comforting shadows. May the spirit of this space hold me in love. May the sense of a found home stay with me, this day and all the days of my life.

NOVEMBER 11

We often speak of a church as being a spiritual home: "If you have come to feel that this is your spiritual home, please consider signing the membership book," for example. Yet we "go home" only once a week—or maybe even once a month. What does it mean to have a spiritual home? What would make it more home-like? What care does it need, what time, what presence? How do we decorate our spiritual home? What are the conditions of ownership?

Do I have a spiritual home? How do I pay the "mortgage" and arrange for the upkeep? ∼

Guide me to create a spiritual home that is homelike. Grant me patience and perseverance, since spiritual homes are located on earth. Grant me energy and spunk, since spiritual homes can ossify with too much devotion. Grant me courage and focus, that my spiritual home will be a priority in my life.

DECADES AGO, a book called *Teaching as a Subversive Activity* arrived on the scene and changed the way a lot of people looked at schools. Educational institutions had become many things to many people—substitute parents, social skills centers, community transformation agents—but in the process schools had sometimes lost sight of their primary mission: to help people learn. Learning is a subversive activity, because it brings into question prevailing ways of thinking and doing things. In the same way, church-going needs to be a subversive activity; people need to remind themselves from time to time why they are there and ask themselves whether or not their institution is going about fulfilling its primary mission.

*Our religious institutions try to accomplish many
things and serve many purposes. In the process, they
may forget that their essential mission has to do with
spiritual transformation. In a pluralistic religious tradition, some institutions become spiritually confused,
leaving members upset and frustrated. Other institutions literally "draw the wagons in," thinking that they
can thereby keep change out. Neither confusion nor
withdrawal, however, will satisfy the needs of people
for the two spiritual dimensions that they seek: inti-
macy and ultimacy. Seekers come seeking a place
where they can be known and accepted for who they
are and connected with others in a deep and abiding
way. They also come for more than family or fellow-
ship, seeking some transcendent, transforming purpose
that will help give meaning to their lives.*

Why do I go to church or synagogue or temple (or why
do I stay away)? ∿

God, stifle the rehearsed response, my normal response,
and let me see and name what it is I need to be a whole
person in a broken world.

NOVEMBER 13

Solitude and silence are powerful ways in which spiritual communities come together in worship. To center down quietly together helps a community feel connected in ways words cannot supply.

Where and when is there time for quiet solitude in my religious community? ∼

Teach me to be still, so that I might hear myself and others.

NOVEMBER 14

Spirituality has more to do with stories than with dogma. When people go to a spiritual community, they are looking for a place in which their stories can be heard and in which the stories of the community can be told.

Where is my life story heard in the community? ∽

Grant me a place to tell my story, and friends to hear and respect it.

NOVEMBER 15

One dynamic quality of a spiritual community is hope. When Thomas Potter built a chapel ten years before John Murray, the Universalist preacher, arrived on American shores, he was acting on hope, not reason. When Olympia Brown decided to enter seminary, against the advice of many, she, too, was acting in the present for a future yet to emerge.

Where is hope expressed in my spiritual community? ∼

Power of the Future, draw me toward you with hope in the present, knowing my own past.

NOVEMBER 16

Ministry is the whole community teaching the whole community what it means to love.

What is my ministry? ∼

Keeper of My Days, renew in me a spirit of compassion and let me act kindly toward others.

NOVEMBER 17

How a community behaves (lives out the values it claims as ultimate) is the real mark of its integrity.

By what values does my spiritual community live? ∼

Strengthen me and my community so that there is no division between what we profess to hold true and how we behave.

NOVEMBER 18

*Each person brings to his or her spiritual community
a map, model, or paradigm of what that community
should be—a map that generally comes from the
person's past experiences or from unexpressed needs.
Some people want a spiritual community to be an
extended family; others are seeking a friendship circle
or social justice organization. It is the creation of a*
shared *map that marks spiritual health.*

What is the ruling map or model I bring to my search for
spiritual community? ⌇

Help me to clarify my needs, hear the needs of others,
and learn how to create a shared meaning and tapestry.

IF SPIRITUAL CONFUSION is a chronic condition of our times, then clarity about our spirituality is the only antidote. For some of us, there is a certain hollowness about communities that establish no boundaries and incorporate the traditions of others without really understanding them at all. It's like the joke someone told about Unitarians going West to convert Native Americans by dancing their dances. What communities such as these lack is not more intelligent people, but deeper people—people who understand spiritual traditions and practices and who realize with humility how complex and difficult it is to enter a culture not one's own.

NOVEMBER 19

Those of us accustomed to the ways of Unitarian Universalism are sometimes surprised when we first encounter the unprogrammed form of worship practiced by Friends (Quakers)—a waiting on God coupled with very brief and succinct spoken messages from the heart. Their way of making decisions— letting the Spirit speak and then reaching shared decisions without a formal vote—can also come as a surprise. As part of this decision-making process, Friends take part in what they call a "Clearness Committee," in which individuals reflect with a supportive group about where the Spirit is leading them. With the invitation to "come discern where God is leading you," Friends seek common ground with words and silence and prayer—with dialogue, in other words—and not with argument or attempts to overwhelm or dazzle the other party with words.

When my spiritual community faces a decision, do I tend to engage in dialogue or resort to argument? ⁓

Settle down, Spirit in my midst, and help me to listen, learn, and grow without fear or the need for self-justification.

NOVEMBER 20

Solitude is the beginning of wisdom.

What is one major spiritual issue with which I have struggled over the years? Have I addressed it in solitude? ∼

In being quiet and alone, let me be honest and clear with myself. Let me not deceive myself with lies. Let me stay here and not be afraid.

When we put into words a problem with which we are wrestling, we take the first step toward "solving" it. A question must be lived into its own responses—or, better put, we can begin to respond to a direction or path only after we have taken the first step.

What path have I already taken? 〜

Step by step lead me into deeper joy and more abundant living.

Solitude is the beginning—but not the end—of discernment and clarity. We need others to help us see ourselves and to suggest paths for us to consider.

Is there one trusted person to whom I might turn for guidance? ∼

For friendship, today I am grateful.

Discussion *(which Unitarian Universalists often perceive to be their strongest characteristic) comes from a Latin word which means "to agitate" (a root also seen in such words as* percussion *and* concussion*). Discussion is much like a game of tennis, an exchange in which people toss opinions back and forth across a net until someone gives up or loses.* Dialogue *comes from the Greek* logos, *meaning "word," and* dia, *meaning "through." Dialogue is about the meaning that emerges between and among people. It is a practice that involves listening more than arguing a point. Though essential, dialogue is seldom practiced, even in spiritual communities that depend on dialogue for health.*

Where have I experienced genuine dialogue? ∿

Be still, my soul, and listen without judging to what others are saying to you and to what you hear yourself saying.

NOVEMBER 24

Spiritual issues have to do with the "big questions" of life that affect us directly, often in times of crisis. Why do I suffer? Why do people act unkindly? How do I face death? The response to such questions is not simply intellectual; rather, it is existential—that is, having to do with the very meaning of one's life.

Do I face the "big questions" of life head-on? ⌣

Sometimes it feels as if life has no purpose, that the good suffer while those who do evil prosper, and that the universe is uncaring. Help me, God, to feel your presence.

There are families who worship together on a weekly basis, attending a church or a synagogue. There are cultures that practice religious devotions that call for prayers five times a day. Individuals practice varying forms of worship and spiritual discipline, both within religious institutions and through personal spiritual rituals and disciplines. Through an institution or on our own, each one of us has the opportunity to explore and deepen our personal relationship with God.

Do I comprehend that a life grounded in spiritual exploration on a regular basis will bring me closer to the Divine? ⌇

Help me to see that the richest and deepest relationship with the Divine comes from my own heart, mind, and soul communicating with the Creator. Encourage me to understand that untold revelations await me.

A PATIENT WAS newly discharged from the hospital to a nursing home. All medical treatments had failed to stop the aggressive growth of cancer in his body. He was told that there was nothing left to do but ensure his comfort. His pastor visited and found the man sitting alone in his room, his face damp with tears. The pastor sat beside him, placing a hand on the man's shoulder, and asked if there was anything he would like to talk about. The man lifted his hand and pointed up, then down, and shrugged his shoulders as if asking a question. The minister repeated his gesture, pointing up, then down, and said to the man, "Are you worried?" The man nodded his head and began to sob.

NOVEMBER 26

"Dying is a wild night and a new road."

—EMILY DICKINSON

Why wait until the hour of death to know the image of God I carry within? ∿

God of New Beginnings, help me see each day as an opportunity to know you and experience your guiding presence.

NOVEMBER 27

*"At the moment of death the sum of all the experi-
ences of life on earth comes to the surface of the
mind—for in the mind are stored all impressions of
past deeds—and the dying man becomes absorbed in
these experiences."*

—SRIMAD BHAGAVATAM

How do I want to live now, so that when I reflect back
on past deeds I find comfort instead of fear? ∿

Gracious God, may my actions ever grow to reflect the
holiness of life and all with whom I share it.

NOVEMBER 28

*"The wise man in the storm prays to God not for
safety from danger but for deliverance from fear. It is
the storm within which endangers him, not the storm
without."*

—RALPH WALDO EMERSON

How do I believe in a loving God against years of messages of a judgmental and punishing God? ∼

Compassionate One, restore my hope, fortify my
courage, and uncloud my vision so that I can move
beyond my fear.

NOVEMBER 29

"I am one of those troubled hearts / Fearing the night, fearing the day."

—RENÉ MARAN

What is it that troubles my heart? ∼

Source of Comfort, be my companion and let me heal from the wounds of uncertainty.

NOVEMBER 30

"If a mighty river has been struck by drought, what hope is there for the waterhole?"

—TALMUD

In times of trouble, where have my strength and hope been found? ⁓

Help me remember that I am connected to you, O God, that the spark of the Divine resides within me. Help me to embrace this partnership.

DECEMBER 1

"The voice said
  You Are Enough
    naked
    crying
    bleeding
    nameless
    starving
    sinful
  You Are Enough"
      —NANCY ORE

How can I release myself from the false belief that I am unworthy and unforgivable? 〜

Surrounded by the love of others, may I find the strength to love myself and give thanks for what is good in my life.

DECEMBER 2

*"How much more authentic a dead Job would be even
after death shaking his fist at the God of pain."*

—ANNA KAMIENSKDA

How much of my pain do I turn toward myself in fear
rather than outward toward the object of my anger?

Let me be free of anger that is fearful or vengeful, carried secretly within my heart. May I learn to express my
anger with the faith that doing so can bring about good.

WHEN WE MAKE of our lives prayers, then we have learned to show reverence for all living beings, and that is the purpose of living: understanding that the Eternal is discovered in the ordinary and revealed there if we have ears to hear and hearts to listen. That which is holy is not necessarily "out there" or even "in here," but among and inside all aspects of life. The Gospel of Thomas teaches us that the holy is in our very midst, even if we cannot always see it with our eyes. In order to experience the holy we must practice wakefulness and teach ourselves to hear, see, and feel.

DECEMBER 3

Working is praying, making love is praying, being alone is praying, washing dishes is praying, reading a bedtime story to a child is praying, spending a moment taking time to observe one small flower is praying, being alone with others is praying, being together with strangers is praying, meditating on a single word is praying, singing is praying, listening is praying, living between the Now and Eternity is praying. If we live well we pray; if we pray we live well.

How is reverence for life "prayer"? ⌣

Slow me down so that I might listen and feel and intuit the holiness of the ordinary, the presence of purpose in my life and in all the lives I share.

DECEMBER 4

Pay very close attention right now to where you are, how you are sitting, what you hear, how you feel, why you are there. Pay attention prayerfully.

What am I feeling right now? ∿

Sometimes I seek solace for my soul outside my soul, but if I listen carefully, I can feel myself restored right now.

DECEMBER 5

All creatures on our planet are worthy. And so one man has made it his practice to feed the birds near his home, especially during the cold winter months. It has taken five months for the birds, mainly chickadees, to wait in a hush for him to fill the bird feeder. They gather in crowds (he calls them "choirs") and watch him fill the feeder. This whole scene has come to feel like worship to the man, because through it he shows reverence to life. As he watches the birds flock to the feeder, he senses that in showing kindness to them, he has fed his soul.

What helps restore my soul? ∿

The presence of God restores my soul and leads me beside still waters. Therefore, I will fear nothing and abide in time and eternity, one foot in each.

DECEMBER 6

Some people make themselves miserable, always seeing the glass half empty instead of half full. Few of us are in a position to judge, however; we may go for days complaining about our situation without so much as noticing the sun or seeing a single crocus beating its way through the earth.

Many life situations are just plain harsh, but what is it that makes one person feel gratitude for whatever small token of meaning he or she has, and another ungrateful and bitter even in the face of plenty? Genes, early childhood training, diet, environment, fate? We may never know the answer, but we can choose how we wish to live: being grateful for the ordinary graces of life that we always find if we look (and paying less attention to life's harshness, which we always seem to discover by looking as well).

What are my "ordinary graces of life"? ～

Giver of Life, who makes the sun shine on everyone, let me look toward the light, that I might be grateful for what I have been given, and less ungrateful for what I lack.

DECEMBER 7

To pray, one must start *praying and not just* think *about praying. Take a few minutes in the morning by yourself and stay in silence—listening, waiting, hearing. If you don't hear anything, don't give up. Pray without ceasing for only a few minutes every day. If you do so and clear out the clutter in your mind and spirit, you will hear. The most amazing story of all is this one: that God speaks to every waiting soul.*

Am I willing to pray every day now and in the days ahead? Let me begin now. ∽

Keep my mind clear and my heart open, that I might hear what others have heard and listen to that still small voice that speaks down the ages.

DECEMBER 8

Look around yourself right now. What do you see?
What do you see that you haven't noticed before?
What do things mean? Keep looking.

How is the ordinary a window to the extraordinary? ∼

God, for the ordinary graces of my life, I give thanks.

DECEMBER 9

Each of our "ordinary lives" is already holy, if we watch over it and keep it well.

In the midst of my life, wherever it might be, where do I encounter the holiness of the ordinary? ◡

Keeper of the Ordinary Days, open my heart to their mystery and purpose, and keep me steadfast in my attention.

ONE OF LIFE'S most difficult lessons is learning how to let go of old ways of behavior, wrongs we perceive others have done to us, simmering angers, hurts, and resentments. Most of us never overcome ourselves, never move beyond the need to justify and protect ourselves. When things fall apart, as they inevitably do eventually, our deepest values and feelings—including all our old resentments—come into play. While letting go in times of trouble strikes at the core of our pretensions of being in control, it can be the process by which life is transformed into love.

DECEMBER 10

*Most of us presume we are immortal; death is what
happens to others, and we are not going to be there
when it happens to us. Yet, as Plato was reported to
have said in summing up his philosophy: practice
dying. We spend a great deal of our lives dying—dying
when we enter school for the first time, dying when
we leave home, dying to old relationships and ways of
behaving. If we have learned how to die, we have
learned a great deal about how to live, about letting
go of ourselves in order to move on. Dying is really
another way of growing, until one day each person
must die to everything and cease to exist on the physical plain.*

What dying experiences have I gone through? ∿

Give me the courage to let go of what is not important
and to die to old resentments and guilt, so that I might
become a whole person.

DECEMBER 11

*When things fall apart—a way of being in the world,
a relationship—then there emerges the possibility of
new ways of being, new relationships, new paths. So
much of our culture teaches us the opposite truth—
that we are here to accumulate goods and persons and
achievements. But like the rich person in one of the
parables of Jesus, who builds up treasures on earth, we
come to a time when everything we have accumulated
is lost and nothing remains—a sobering but truthful
wisdom.*

How much of my life has been spent accumulating
things? ∼

It is not things, but the *love* of things, that may dominate
my life. Teach me to live simply and to show a spirit of
giving to others.

DECEMBER 12

Holding on, letting go. These are two ways of being in the world—not necessarily diametrical opposites, but opposites held in creative tension. We can really appreciate only what we have learned is mortal, for then we value it all the more given the brevity. And we can love only when we have learned to let go and welcome others' freedom and uniqueness, ceasing to make them into our own images.

To what am I holding on as if my life depended on it? ～

Lord, help me to relax and to let go of my wish to control what happens. May I grow in my capacity to accept what life brings.

DECEMBER 13

Saying good-bye to what we truly love is one of life's most painful experiences. And yet, even during such times, we know that we would not mourn so deeply the loss if we had not first loved so much. It is a troubling truth we learn: Those who love most live most deeply—and feel losses all the more. In that riddle is the mystery of being human.

When I have said good-bye to someone I love, what has brought me strength? ∼

O God, let something remain of all my good-byes to strengthen and nourish my soul now.

DECEMBER 14

Kairos *is a Greek word for "new," roughly meaning new life arising out of the old. If we have lived well, loved often, and had to let go, sometimes we find* kairos—*new life emerging, the stone rolled away so that we might see the light of day.*

When have I been a witness to *kairos*? ∼

Help me to let go and say good-bye, so that what comes afterward may hold on to me and say hello.

DECEMBER 15

Coming to an end is really coming to another beginning. And as we discover looking back, in every beginning is the end.

What new beginning do I envision for myself? ⌒

In the silence of my heart, help me to see the new which is even now emerging within me, and let me greet it kindly and with courage.

DECEMBER 16

May the presence of shalom, *of peace, be with us all
as we travel the open road, and may love and strength
be with us and with all those we love.*

In whose love am I sheltered right now? ⁓

Peace be unto me. Peace be unto others. Peace be with
all beings, great and small.

LIFE IS OFTEN seen as a journey. None of us knows the end; nor are we sure of the beginning. All we have is now as we step into the unknown. But we do know other travelers along the way who bring us comfort and joy. Sometimes we can glance back and see those who follow after us; at other times we can look ahead and catch a brief view of those who go before. We cannot fully determine the future; nor can we change the past. But we can walk the present road with dignity and integrity, and we can walk with others, our comrades, along the way.

DECEMBER 17

Our highways have become a battle ground in the bumper-sticker war: "S--T HAPPENS" versus "GRACE HAPPENS." We hurtle our vehicles, ever larger and more powerful, down highways at increasing speeds, and we externalize our worldview to distract others from the task at hand. Someone should do research on the religious implications of bumper stickers as they relate to driving tendencies, but "GRACE HAPPENS" cars would probably come out on top. When grace happens, we are healed. Our hearts are made whole, our lives restored. Only say the word—only send a grace-filled moment—and I shall be healed.

Am I open to being healed? ⌣

Divine Healer, help my heart to be whole. Help my brokenness to be healed. Help my soul to be open. Steer me from my own ambition, from my own proclamations of self-importance, and restore a simple faith that grace can happen.

DECEMBER 18

A man was sitting on top of his house watching the floodwaters rise. Another man came by in a rowboat and offered him a ride to higher ground. He replied, "No thanks. God promised to save me." The other man shrugged and went on. As the waters rose further, a helicopter came by overhead. The crew threw down a rope and told the man to hang on while they pulled him up. Again he refused, saying that God had promised to save him.

The waters continued to rise, and the man was swept away and drowned. On arriving in heaven, he demanded to know why God had not saved him as promised. God replied, "I sent a rowboat and a helicopter. What more did you want?"

Did a rowboat come in answer to my prayers? ∼

Help me to see the presence of grace and the many helping hands in my life; help me to know that I do not walk life alone.

DECEMBER 19

Let me see the road less traveled and not be afraid to
take it, nor be envious of those who take common
roads of security and ease, understanding that nothing
is secure and little that is worthwhile is easy. Help me
to recognize others who try the road less traveled and
need comforting as much as I do.

When I picture myself looking back at the road I have
been on, what does that road look like? ∼

Give me strength to continue the journey, knowing dis-
appointments but also knowing and gaining strength
from friends of your beloved community.

DECEMBER 20

"Power is starting your chainsaw on the first pull."

—WEBSTER KITCHELL

What are the tools for my work in the world? Are they in good condition; will they work when needed? What outside myself powers them? ⁓

O God, thank you for those gifts and inner resources that ease my way.

DECEMBER 21

"You must always keep in mind that a path is only a path. If you feel you should not follow it, you must not stay with it under any conditions. To have such clarity, you must lead a disciplined life.... Look at every path closely and deliberately."

—CARLOS CASTENEDA

What is the step right in front of me that I am called to take? ∿

Help me to remember that a journey of a thousand miles begins with one step. Although it is nice to have a vision of where my path is leading, the long view is not necessary to taking the step that is right in front of me.

DECEMBER 22

*In reflecting on his experience of meeting Thomas
Potter and preaching the first Universalist sermon in
his chapel in 1770, Rev. John Murray noted, "I was
astonished; I was lost in wonder, in love, and in
praise; I saw, as evidently as I could see any object ...
that the good hand of God was in all these things."*

In what events or moments have I experienced a sense
of transcendence, of some power or energy beyond my
own leading me into uncharted territories? ⌇

Guiding Power, may I remember with gratitude your
hands on my life, leading me by beauty and light where
sometimes I would rather not go. Keep me on the path
and help me to remember that I do not walk alone.

DECEMBER 23

When we begin something new, we always carry with us the baggage of the past—whether from a former relationship, an old job, or memories of friendships or adversaries. Making a new start entails integrating the past, acknowledging its influence without becoming enslaved to it.

What relationships do I cling to from the past? What am I afraid of repeating in the future? ⌒

I will make peace with my past by finding a place in my heart for the sweet memories of friends I have made. I will also work on forgiving myself and others for mistakes or transgressions so that I can move on with my life.

THERE IS A STORY told about a Zen master and his student. The student is asked to fix a crack in the wall. He does so by putting plaster over it. The master returns, looks at the wall, and then slaps the student on the head, saying, "If you want to repair the crack, first you must knock down the wall."

All you need to begin with is yourself. Spend a few moments every day in prayer or meditation, writing down notes to yourself. If you prefer to read a Bible passage or other sacred literature before settling down, do not tackle too much reading; instead, read as if you were feeding your soul, which you are.

All the rest is discipline.

DECEMBER 24

Most of the time we put plaster over the broken parts of our relationships, and then wonder why they never seem to be fixed. Sometimes it is necessary to fix the broken parts by starting over and making them whole.

What doesn't seem to get fixed in my life? ⌣

When things fall apart, help me not to react quickly and try to fix them, but let them fall and see what results.

DECEMBER 25

There are moments in religious history when something out of the ordinary enters time and makes a new beginning out of what seemed a hopeless cause.

When have I felt something very powerful and different entering my life when I least expected it? ∿

Keep me open to the possibilities of new beginnings and the power of the future coming into my present.

DECEMBER 26

Sometimes we need to be jolted out of our life pat-
terns so that we can wake up and change. It would
be easier if we had the inner strength to see what
changes are needed and carry them out. But most of
us change when we are faced with the necessity.

What has caused major changes in my life? ⌣

Changing, growing Creator, awaken me to the change
already taking place and teach me how to make such
transitions with grace and wisdom.

DECEMBER 27

It has been said that the teacher appears when the student is ready. The lessons needed to live are presented to us every day, but we only act on them when we are ready.

When have my life teachers appeared on the scene? ∿

Keep me alert and awake to life and the possibilities of growth, so that I am not asleep when my teachers come.

DECEMBER 28

"So we beat on, boats against the current, borne back ceaselessly into the past."

—F. SCOTT FITZGERALD

What past life issues keep returning for me to solve?

Help me to ride with the current and know the ease of it all.

DECEMBER 29

"On action alone be thy interest, never on its fruits."

—BHAGAVAD GHITA

What stops me from starting on a new path? ∿

May my fear be stilled long enough for me to look at the next step I must take and not be made anxious by the complexities of life. The first step is all that can be asked of any person.

DECEMBER 30

"In the middle of the journey of our life I came to myself within a dark wood where the straight way was lost."

—DANTE ALIGHIERI

Have I ever felt completely lost in life? ∽

Help me to remember that every person feels lost at times in their lives and I am not alone, but part of a company of strangers who have made a journey not unlike mine. Let me draw strength from them.

DECEMBER 31

Life is a bumpy road.

—THE BUDDHA'S FIRST NOBLE TRUTH

How well am I riding out the bumps in life? Am I living with the reality of the bumps, denying them, or being bounced around by them? ∽

"May I be well. May I be happy and peaceful. May no harm come to me. May I be freed from greed, selfishness, and jealousy. May I be able to face life's problems with patience, courage, and understanding."

—BUDDHIST INVOCATION

ACKNOWLEDGMENTS

Many thanks to the Fund for Unitarian Universalism and the Pennsylvania Universalist Convention, especially their president, Nelson Simonson, for supporting me as I wrote this book and others. I am indebted also to Juliet Wagner Donner of Lewisburg, Pennsylvania, who gave me a gift of *Day Unto Day*, the last Unitarian daily devotional guide, published by the American Unitarian Association in the late nineteenth century. And with gratitude to Mary Benard, Skinner House editor, who helped me to give shape and purpose to this book. And a very special word of thanks to my friends whose writings and insights are woven into the very fabric of this book: Kathy "Kate" Seitz Bortner, Patricia Carol, Ellen Chulak, Janelle Curlin-Taylor, Florence Gelo, Paul Hull, Karen Kromer-Lynch, Michael Masters, Lowell McMullin, Stan Sears, and Jeff Taylor. Your words and lives have enriched mine more than you will ever know. And finally, with love and gratitude to my partner, Cynthia, and my son, Jonathan, in whose love I have grown beyond my limited capacities.

—J.C.M.